# IT'S LIFE AND DEATH, BUT NOT AS YOU KNOW IT!

# IT'S LIFE AND DEATH, BUT NOT AS YOU KNOW IT!

## From the Unbelievable to the *Bizarre*

**TRICIA J. ROBERTSON**

www.whitecrowbooks.com

It's Life And Death, But Not As You Know It!



Published in the United States of America and the United Kingdom by
White Crow Books; an imprint of White Crow Productions Ltd.



For information, contact White Crow Books by e-mail: info@whitecrowbooks.com.
Cover Design by Astrid@Astridpaints.com
Interior design by Velin@Perseus-Design.com

A CIP catalogue record for this book is available from the British Library

Paperback ISBN: 978-1-78677-143-8
eBook ISBN: 978-1-78677-144-5

Non-Fiction / Body, Mind & Spirit / Parapsychology / Unexplained phenomena

www.whitecrowbooks.com

## Praise for
## *It's Life And Death, But Not As You Know It!*

~

"Who better to take readers on an exploration of the paranormal than Tricia Robertson, an experienced researcher of spontaneous phenomena as well as a dedicated investigator of mediumship under test conditions? Her previous books dealt impressively with the evidence for life after death that she had either experienced personally or had gathered from those who had it thrust upon them through unsought encounters with the unknown. These meaningful events appeared to be signals to them from loved ones who had died. Her latest book takes readers much deeper into the paranormal, providing a wealth of testimony from well-qualified eyewitnesses to phenomena that are, quite literally, beyond belief. Robertson has condensed some of her own work with the very best reports, from more than a century of psychical research around the world, into very readable accounts that require no special knowledge of the subject on the part of her readers. The extraordinary events described in its pages will challenge many of her readers' assumptions about a wide variety of paranormal phenomena and, indeed, the very nature of reality. Interaction with the spirits of the dead may be a possible explanation in some cases, but others appear to be almost impossible to explain. Robertson leaves it to her readers to make up their own minds, though I suspect most will be satisfied simply to enjoy the entertainment value of the astonishing reports she shares and leave the speculation to others".

~ **Roy Stemman,** journalist and author of *Surgeon From Another World and The Big Book of Reincarnation.*

Writers and mythmakers have long created stories portraying what happens to us when we die. Novelist, theologian, philosopher, and psychical researcher Stafford Betty has broken new ground with *The Afterlife Therapist.* This fast-paced, humanly credible afterlife story is based on what science has to say about our conscious survival after death. The picture Betty provides is one of continued challenges, replete with 'heavenly' and 'hellish' potentials. For readers in pandemic times, the vision encoded in this book is most welcome. So, stand aside, Dante

"Fascinating and thought-provoking. Tricia is an inspired teacher and this book captures the unique style that I'm sure she applied in the very popular courses in Psychical Research she ran for six years for the Department of Adult and Continuing Education (DACE) at the University of Glasgow in conjunction with Professor Archie Roy.

Whereas in her first two books she covered the evidence for different forms of mediumship as well as reincarnation, poltergeist activity, paranormal healing cases, and hauntings, in this book she takes a different tack.

"Tricia covers a huge amount of ground with details that even those familiar with the field of paranormal research will find fascinating. Most of the cases raise questions about the as yet undocumented powers of the mind, a subject at the core of serious psychical research as well as consciousness studies.

"Anyone claiming to investigate the paranormal or to be involved with mediumship needs to understand the implications of the studies she cites on clairvoyance, precognition, retrocognition, as well as thoughtography, all of which do not appear to involve spirit contact.

Tricia makes it clear that she remains firmly in the camp of survival of consciousness, but she treats reader with respect – giving him/her first an overview, and frequently details of the best cases, and then says "It is up to you now to make up your mind about all of this or perhaps investigate this further for yourself".

"Tricia has done a sterling job of succinctly summarising the cases and presenting the material in an interesting way. And, fortunately, she has maintained her lovely conversational style with frequent anecdotes, often involving investigators personally known to her.

"Once again, she has made a wonderful contribution to the White Crow Books library of timeless classics".

~ **Victor and Wendy Zammit,** authors of *A Lawyer Presents the Evidence for the Afterlife and 'The Afterlife Report'.*

"Lawyer Alan Murdie recently concluded on the basis of evidence recently published in the journal *American Psychologist* that 2018 could well be the year that parapsychological research was finally accepted by mainstream science. However, university research has been preoccupied with finding a so-called repeatable lab-experiment and as yet tells us virtually nothing about the true nature of psychic phenomena. For this the reader would need to turn to the cases presented so clearly and concisely by Tricia Robertson. Her book covers, along with her own experiences, the outstanding cases of classical phenomena with a particular emphasis on mediumship cases. Although I would differ as to the explanations of some of the cases, her last chapter summing up all the evidence is both daring and thought provoking. It should be read by anyone trying to make sense of psychic phenomena".

~ **Adrian Parker,** Professor in Psychology, licensed clinical psychologist, University of Gothenburg.

# Contents

## Foreword

This is an unusual book. It is encyclopaedic in its scope as it deals with various "unbelievable to bizarre" phenomena including mediumship, electronic voice phenomenon and much more; particularly interesting as these phenomena are found in different types of psychic individuals.

*It's Life And Death, But Not As You Know It!* is fluently written and easy to read, covering as it does the whole field of paranormal phenomena, describing some of her own experiences and how they have appeared in the life and work of a great number of individuals, such as Arigo to the Gold Leaf Lady, to mention only two. It presents quite a fascinating account of what has happened in real life and been critically observed – and sometimes tested – by a great number of individuals. The emphasis is on spontaneous phenomena – the real stuff – as my late colleague Dr. Karlis Osis, director of research of the American Society of Psychical Research, used to refer to them. Namely, the emphasis is on spontaneous, real life phenomena.

This book reveals how exceptionally widely read Tricia Robertson is. She also includes paranormal accounts related to some major disasters such as the sinking of the "unsinkable" Titanic, and the disaster of the famous (now mostly forgotten?) airship R101.

In the realm of electronic voice phenomena, Konstantin Raudive, Hans Otto König and Anabela Cardoso are not forgotten, nor is the very strange thoughtography of Ted Serios.

Congratulations Tricia, you have written one more highly interesting book.

Erlendur Haraldsson PhD, Professor emeritus of Psychology, Reykjavík, Iceland. Author of *The Departed Among the Living: An Investigative Study of Afterlife Encounters* and *Towards the Unknown: Memoir of a Psychical Researcher*

# Introduction

Life is a funny old thing, full of contradictions and confusion for those of us participating on this journey.

We are complex beings with intelligence, physical needs and emotions, but which has the biggest influence over us? Physically we need to survive by eating, sleeping, keeping disease at bay and forming at least one friendship for our emotional needs. But it would appear that we also have some kind of spiritual need, asking questions of ourselves and our place in the world.

One question might be, 'What can we learn about our place in life?' Another, 'What personal talents, hidden or otherwise, might we have?' And the big question is, 'Why do we exist at all?' The big question I cannot begin to answer.

We may be floundering over all of these questions as to the curiosity of life, and so have many eminent scientific thinkers through history.

In his 1898 address before the British Association at Bristol, Professor William Crookes said,

> Those who assume that we are now acquainted with all, or nearly all, or even with any assignable proportion, of the forces that work in the universe, show a limitation of conception which ought to be impossible in an age when the widening of the circle of our definite knowledge does but reveal the proportionally widening circle of our blank, absolute indubitable ignorance.

Regardless of the mystery of our being, the reality is that we are here and hopefully we can enjoy the journey. It may also be of value to examine the world around us in pursuit of some kind of understanding of our place in the Universe.

So what hidden abilities might we hold while we are alive? You may be surprised as you read though this book.

Aside from conjecturing about physical life, what about the demise of the physical body? We now have to ask another question: is there any evidence that our consciousness survives physical death?

Philosophers, writers and poets have thought deeply about this throughout time and asked the same question.

Socrates reasoned, 'Death is one of two things. Either it is annihilation and the dead have no consciousness of anything, or, as we are told, it is really a change: a migration of the soul from this place to another'.

Shakespeare's Hamlet said:

> But that we dread of something after death
> The undiscovered country from whose bourn
> No traveller returns, puzzles the will
> And makes us rather bear those ills we have
> Than fly to others that we know naught of.

Science is wonderful, or rather I should say 'known' science is wonderful, but it does not comprehensively cover many avenues of pragmatic human experience. Unfortunately this can in many cases lead to closed minds, especially when it comes to psychical research and matters of survival of consciousness.

Prime Minister William E. Gladstone, 1809-1898, thought so when he wrote:

> I have always thought that scientific men run too much in a groove. They do noble work in their special line of research, but they are often indisposed to give any attention to matters which seem to conflict with their established modes of thought. Indeed, they not infrequently attempt to deny that into which they have never inquired, not sufficiently realising the fact that there may possibly be forces in nature of which they know nothing.

This is especially true in the case of psychic phenomena: some people just 'know' that these things cannot happen and pontificate about the absurdity of it from a perspective of ignorance and predisposed bias.

The Dutch philosopher Spinoza said, 'A free man is one who lives under the guidance of reason, who is not led by fear, but who directly desires that which is good'.

The important word here is reason. In my opinion the loudmouth uninformed sceptic who has not really examined any of the best evidence, or indeed has chosen to ignore it, is not being at all reasonable or rational. Another ploy for the anxious sceptic is to cite a very weak example of a particular phenomenon leading him to declare that the whole subject is nonsense. This is similar to throwing the baby out with the bath water.

I would agree that some of the outlandish topics, which I address in this book, may on first appearance not seem to be at all 'reasonable', but before forming an opinion it would be advantageous to read the available evidence.

This book is written for the person in the street who desires to read about credible and authentic evidence concerning our latent talents as human beings along with evidence that strongly points to the survival of human consciousness and personality after death.

In my first two books, I wrote about fairly well recognised topics including poltergeist activity, drop-in communicators, reincarnation, out of body experiences, various forms of mediumship, healing and automatic writing.

In this book I will take you on a journey of seeming madness, from the hard to believe to the bizarre, which may lead you to think, 'Now the woman has just gone too far'. I will guide you through events, which sound downright crazy, weird and impossible, completely beyond your boggle threshold, but if you examine and digest the evidence presented, you will be in a better position to form an opinion about them.

The way of science is to follow the evidence. In this country there are two accepted forms of evidence – mathematical and scientific – where the result of, say, adding two and two together will always make four, and evidence as in a court of law, beyond reasonable doubt. Pragmatic evidence, as with much of paranormal activity, falls into the second category.

If these things actually happen – which they do – then we, as human beings, are even more fascinating than one could ever have imagined. I will hopefully open your mind by providing you with interesting and sometimes bizarre examples of abilities that you may have while still alive, and dead. The evidence provided should help you to answer at least one of the earlier questions, 'Is there any evidence which leads us to believe that there is life after death?' Or, probably more correctly, 'Does the essence of who we are, our consciousness, our intellect, our memories and personality continue after the demise of the physical body?'

I will introduce you a world of possibilities, which you must evaluate for yourself, making sure that your assessment includes taking heed of the actual evidence.

This book also seeks to illustrate the difficulties that can, at times, beset psychical researchers in their quest for truth: Sometimes in a humorous way and at other times, not so much.

My books are meant to be an introduction to many subjects within the broad spectrum of 'the paranormal'.

# 1

# Mediumship And Consciousness

A medium purports to connect with the mind (or consciousness) of a deceased person and in doing so gain veridical information, which is then passed to the sitter who has come for a reading. I have studied these matters long enough to know that *in the best cases* the information delivered by the mediums displays the knowledge, idiosyncrasies, memories and personality of the deceased. This being the case the sensible person would have to proffer some kind of argument or theory to explain the accurate information that is provided within this scenario. It is no good in simply saying that these things cannot happen, therefore it is all fraud and misperception and I am having nothing to do with these distasteful ideas. That is not a rational or educated opinion based on the evidence gathered over the last 100 years or so.

A theory in any avenue of interest is just that – a theory, which has to be tested to see if it fits all of the facts. The 'theory' that mediumship communication is all cold reading, misinterpretation and lucky guessing simply does not wash, as it most certainly does not fit all of the facts in the better cases. The 'cold reading theory' also does not fit with many good experimental results, especially as many, including my own, are carried out in double, or even triple, blind conditions. Although I am only dealing with good, evidential, cases, I have to concede that a high percentage of modern mediumship information given to sitters can indeed be non-evidential and mediocre at best. But this does not negate the value of the best examples.

## *Secondly: consciousness*

Materialists think that the brain is the source of consciousness and when the body dies all 'real time' consciousness goes with it. Although there are competing theories in this matter the truth is that as far as we know, no one on this planet can reliably describe consciousness or accurately point to where it resides within the human body. It is not just 'awareness' of one's surroundings although that is of course part of it. A worm may be aware of its surroundings but I doubt that it can, for example, hold a séance producing materialisation or generate poltergeist activity. But regardless of what consciousness actually is or where it lies we can on occasion observe and document the use of an individual's consciousness and how it links with or affects others, whether they are alive or dead. This we can do by studying people with unusual abilities. The following is one example.

## *Gerard Croiset*

It is strange to think that some people seem to have the ability to tap into the consciousness of other people who are still alive, but they can. By this I do not just mean ordinary telepathic experiments with twins or other people or just the feeling of knowing what another person is thinking, but by studying people with very unusual talents. One such person was the Dutch clairvoyant Gerard Croiset. We usually think of the word clairvoyant in relation to a medium contacting a deceased person, but in Croiset's case he was indeed repeatedly able to tap into the consciousness of other people *including* those who had passed over *and* those still alive.

Croiset was sometimes called upon by the Dutch police to determine the whereabouts of a missing person whether they were presumed alive or dead, or to gain information about them. Croiset was also utilised by the Dutch police over many years to solve cases of theft and murder by using his amazing abilities.

Many people think that the evidential results produced from different avenues of psychical research have a sell by date – but they do not. A fact is a fact, regardless of the time in which it was witnessed and documented. When someone as spectacular as Croiset has been researched and found to be the 'real deal' his abilities should not be forgotten. However, they often are. In this day and age when consciousness is a 'buzz word' I think that the examples of Croiset's abilities are more important than ever and they should give us further food for thought.

As to the man himself, he was a Dutch grocer who, in the mid 1940s at the age of thirty-four, began to develop clairvoyance. Whether this was a natural development or a concentrated effort by himself I know not but the subsequent results speak for themselves. We are indeed fortunate in that his abilities came to the attention of Professor Tenhaeff, Director of the Parapsychology Institute in Utrecht, who systematically documented many of Croiset's cases.

We may never have known about this man's work if it were not for Jack Harrison Pollack who published detailed translations from the *Dutch Journal of Parapsychology*, Tenhaeff's scholarly books and Dutch police records, in his book *Croiset, The Clairvoyant.*

It is worth noting that Croiset never charged a penny for the use of his extraordinary abilities. So much so that, even when he was consulted by the police, he insisted on paying for his own travel expenses. He also declined to use his talents for his own financial gain such as stock market dealings, predictions, horse racing or any other sort of gambling, although he did once visit a racecourse and picked the winners of the first four races! This did not sit well with him and he never repeated that experience again. He wanted to use his paranormal abilities for the good of mankind. He is quoted as saying, 'I have a gift from God which I don't understand. I can't use it just to make money from it for myself. If I do, I may lose it'.

His ability appears to challenge our scientific theories of time and space. Not only could he 'tune in' to missing people alive or dead, regardless of distance, but also he could receive impressions of things that happened in the past and in some cases predict the future. He stated, 'The past, present and future are difficult to separate for me'.

When the respected Dr J. B. Rhine of Duke University visited Holland in 1951 he offered to test Croiset's abilities using his experimental Zener cards, Croiset declined the offer saying, 'I respect your work very much, Dr Rhine but I do not like just to guess cards. I have to be emotionally involved in a case, such as that of a missing child or somebody in trouble'.

That statement seems to be key in paranormal phenomena in that emotion seems to play a crucial part. I find it interesting in that emotion, as far as I can tell, is something that we cannot easily measure. Granted, you can tell when someone is angry but you cannot really accurately measure the anger. It is the same with love – you cannot sit a test to display how much you really love a person. Emotion does seem to act as some sort of carrier wave underlying psychic phenomena although at this time we cannot really explain it or its modus operandi.

## *Croiset's abilities*

In October 1959 the daughter of an American professor from Kansas disappeared from a hospital in Topeka where she had been receiving treatment for a nervous breakdown. The professor, a former Rhodes scholar, was a very reserved gentleman with a string of academic qualifications to his name and was not a man to deviate from a path of anything that would not appear to be totally acceptable and 'respectable' within his social group. However, when after a month and a half there was still no official word as to his daughter's whereabouts he decided to contact Croiset to see if he could help. 'I thought it was worth a try', he said at the time.

On December 11, he contacted Professor Tenhaeff in Utrecht to inquire if Croiset had ever solved a case over the telephone. The reply was, 'Sometimes'. Arrangements were made for the missing girl's father to call the Parapsychological Institute the next day at 3:00 p.m. when he would be able to speak to Croiset through an interpreter. As Tenhaeff spoke excellent English he ended up being the interpreter on that day. The conversation lasted twenty-two minutes.

> Croiset: Is there a river near the hospital where your daughter had been?
> Professor: Yes. The Kansas River runs close by.
> Croiset: I see your daughter running over a large lawn and then crossing a viaduct. Now I see her at a place where there are stores, and near them a large body of water with landing stages and many small boats. I see her riding there in a lorry and in a big red car.
> Professor: Is she still alive?
> Croiset: Yes, don't worry. You will hear something definite at the end of six days.

It was then arranged that the professor would phone Tenhaeff and Croiset six days after this conversation. On that day the professor reached out his hand to pick up the telephone in his living room, as he did so he stopped short, as he was astounded to see his daughter sitting on the sofa. After the initial shock he phoned Utrecht to give them the good news. On subsequent questioning it was found that everything that Croiset had said was 100% correct.

Many of Croiset's cases are very complex but I am sticking to simple ones to give you examples of his abilities. The next case does not have the same happy ending.

In September 1960 a stranger telephoned Croiset at midnight from the small rural town of Hedel, some 85 miles away. He was calling on behalf of his neighbour whose seven-year-old son was missing. The family were distraught, as they did not know if he had been kidnapped or had got lost. The caller pleaded with Croiset, 'Please, can you help us?' Although Croiset was still a bit drowsy having been roused from his bed he replied, 'I see a boy walking along a wide road. Something frightened him. There is water. I see him no longer. There is a mist over the water. I am sorry, the child drowned. His fishing rod lies near him. I have an image of a tunnel – search where I said immediately'. Croiset went back to sleep but an hour later the phone rang again and it was yet another neighbour who was unaware of the first call, this neighbour was phoning from the home of the boy's parents. The Burgomaster of Hedel was also with them. Croiset now had a clearer impression, 'I see three dykes ... they must be roads ... coming together ... I see the tunnel again ... and near it a small store house with a steel door. I also see a culvert. There I have my greatest emotion. I see a slope of stone, a lot of concrete and new cement on a bridge. Near that small tunnel you will find that child lying in water ... his fishing rod is near him'.

Burgomaster Van Werken subsequently wrote in his official report, 'In daylight we again started dragging near a small tunnel, only a few metres away was a culvert below the main state road. They dragged in front of the culvert during the night but not in it. When we found the child – his fishing rod was indeed near him. The boy was completely stiffened so we can assume that he had been dead for twelve hours or so, Mr Croiset gave exact details of where the child would be found'.

So far we have seen that Gerard Croiset has provided information about one person who was still alive and, sadly, one who had died. The next example is even stranger.

Tenhaeff designed an experiment to test Croiset to see if he had any ability in the field of precognition. His first set of trials were so successful that the experiment was subsequently repeated nearly four-hundred times, using rigid controls, by scientists from Germany, Holland, Austria, Italy and Switzerland.

The experimental protocol required that a chair number be selected at random as the target for a forthcoming public meeting. Croiset was either told the number or indeed he sometimes selected the number himself. He could then describe with amazing accuracy the chief characteristics of the person who would occupy that seat, e.g. his/her sex, personality, appearance etc.

There was no perceived difference in the experimental results between his seat number being self-selected or a chosen number being supplied to him.

Here is a typical example.

> On January 6, 1957, Tenhaeff travelled to the Parapsychology Institute in Utrecht. He was accompanied by a Miss Louwerens, Professor L.H. Bretschneider, a biologist, and Professor J. A. Smit, a physicist.
>
> Croiset was there and was handed a seating plan for a meeting that was to be held in twenty-five days time in the home of a Mrs C. V. T, a woman from The Hague, who was unknown to both Croiset and Tenhaeff. The only thing known at that time by everyone present was that thirty chairs would be set out for the experiment. At that time the guest list had not been formalised by those given that task. The experimenters were never involved in the selection of the guest list.
>
> The experimenters turned on a tape to record the proceedings. Croiset selected chair number 9 as the chosen target and then he stated,
>
> 1. 'On Friday February 1, in the home of a lady in the Hague, a cheerful middle-aged little woman will sit in chair number 9. She is very interested in caring for children'.
>
> 2. Between 1928 and 1930 I see many of her footsteps were taken near the Kurhaus and Strassburger's Circus in Scheveningen.
>
> 3. When she was a little girl she had many experiences in a district where there was lots of cheese making ... I see a farm on fire where some animals burned to death.

4. I also see three boys ... one has a build like mine. He has a job in some oversees area. It seems to me like a British territory.

5. Has she been looking at a picture of a Maharajah? I see somebody from India ... he is wearing the dress of an inhabitant of that country ... a turban with a large jewel.

6. Did she ever drop a handkerchief into a cage with wild animals? I see a piece of cloth fall. These animals ... and they look like lions ... tear the cloth to pieces.

7. I also see a scrap of paper with the number six on top. At first it was five but she has changed it to a six. This just happened and she had many arguments about it.

8. Has she also recently soiled her hands on an old fashioned paint-box? I see a box with small tablets of paint ... did she hurt herself slightly with that? ... the middle finger of her right hand'.

Author's note: It seems to me that when he appears to be asking questions he is really just thinking aloud. After all, he absolutely knows that the experimenters do not know the answers as no one present even knows who the target subject will be. Anyway, back to his statements.

9. Has she also recently been visited by a woman friend about 44 years old, not very tall, well built, stout, with dark hair, and wearing a dress with several large pleats in front? Did this woman talk to her about sexual problems and did she advise her friend to visit a psychiatrist?

10. Has she experienced strong emotions about the opera Falstaff? Is that the first opera she ever saw?

11. Did her father receive a gold medal for services he rendered?

12. Has she taken a little girl to the dentist? And did this visit cause a lot of commotion? I can almost say that this will happen on Friday, February 1, 1957'.

(It did transpire that this happened on the same day as the proposed meeting.)

The tape was played back and Croiset was asked if he had any further impressions. Yes he did. On point 2 he had the impression of a man of about 45, very emotional and sensitive – his wife did not understand him. They were separated ... this man had affairs with other women and his wife had affairs with other men.

On point 4 he now got the impression that one of these boys was dead. His death had something to do with the (German) occupation of 'our' country.

He admitted that the image of a lion on point 6 was probably symbolic and he said, 'I once compared a mesmerist to a lion tamer and the public to the lions. When the lion tamer gets too close to the lions, they devour him'.

Regarding point 12 he stated, 'I suddenly saw my grown-up daughter as a child. When she was five years old I took her to the dentist. She refused to open her mouth and stayed with the dentist for several hours'.

The experimenters transcribed the original statements and made forty copies. The supplementary data was not copied, as it would only be checked with the person who eventually sat on seat number 9.

The appointed day of February 1st arrived. The experimenter responsible for negotiations at the home of Mrs C. V. T. had not been given any information about the statements made by Croiset.

On the night of the experiment more professors and doctors were called in to oversee the randomisation of seat numbers. No one but Croiset and the original experimenters knew that seat number 9 was the target. Each person was now in possession of a random seat number in which they had to sit. Once everyone was seated they each received a copy of Croiset's statements. They were then instructed to tick only the statements that could apply to them. Cutting the methodology short – the outcome was as follows: There were 30 people in the room and the results showed that virtually none of the statements applied to twenty-nine of them. The only person who could accept a large majority of the statements was the woman in seat number 9. This lady was a Mrs M. D.

Author's note: As an aside, I noted from the report that when the people entered the experimentation room they were given instructions not to TOUCH any chair that was not their appointed number. I found that curious and interesting. I wondered if they would they have left a trail of some sort, such as a bloodhound might follow from a scent? An impression – a psychic link, perhaps. Who knows?

The results were as follows:

1. Mrs M. D. was 42 years old, a cheerful active vivacious woman who admitted a tremendous interest in child care. As predicted.

2. Her parents were divorced. Her father, a sensitive emotional man, worked in the Netherlands East Indies. When on leave he often took her to the circus in Scheveningen. And indeed both parents maintained intimate relations with another woman and man respectively. All as predicted between original statements and additional information.

3. The lady often visited farms as a child but the chief product was butter, not cheese. The statement about a farm where animals were burned to death can be best explained by an experience of Mrs D's son. The boy worked on a farm where he witnessed a horse being killed by lightning. He was profoundly affected by it for a long time. So, not exactly as predicted.

4. Her husband had two brothers, one who volunteered to fight in Indonesia although he only got as far as Singapore, and another who died in a concentration camp. This second brother had a build similar to Croiset. Very similar to prediction.

5. A few days before this experimental meeting Mrs D. had been looking at a picture of a Yogi in a book. She then had a conversation with her son about it and the Hindu Magi. Similar to prediction.

6. Mrs D. insisted that she could not place this image, but Croiset insisted that it would become clear when she read statement number 9.

7. Between January 26, and February 1, after Mrs D. had been balancing her housekeeping book it was discovered that she had put a five where there should have been a six which caused a major quarrel with her husband as the books did not balance. As predicted.

8. In early January Mrs D's children were 'messing around' with an old-fashioned paint-box, the kind with small paint tablets. She wanted to get rid of it and in so doing got her hands and a towel covered in paint. About the same time she cut the middle finger of her right hand on a tin of vegetables; this might indicate that Croiset seemed to combine the two images. A slightly mixed prediction, but correct in essence.

9. Mrs D. confirmed that she had been speaking with a woman friend who was not very tall, well built, stout, had dark hair and often wore a dress with large pleats. They did discuss sexual problems and Mrs D. had referred the woman to a mesmerist. So far, spot on.
   However we have to address the additional information that was provided. Croiset spoke about a handkerchief and lions. On further interview, when Croiset heard the name of the mesmerist he said, 'this man is not trustworthy in sexual matters; a mesmerist or psychiatrist must know how to remain aloof from his patients. Otherwise 'the lions will devour him'. When asked what that had to do with a handkerchief he referred to a game that he had played as a child; 'Handkerchief hidden, telling forbidden'. Saying, 'No one should be told what happens between a woman and her mesmerist or psychiatrist'.

10. It proved to be that Mrs D. was a professional opera singer and the first opera in which she sang was Falstaff. She had also fallen in love with the tenor in it. As predicted.

11. When her father retired he had received a gold, inscribed, cigarette case. Croiset thought it was a gold medal for services rendered.

12. Mrs D's small daughter had a cavity in her front tooth. On the day of the experiment she took her to the dentist. The child was very frightened of the pain and suffered during the visit. This was as predicted, even down to the exact date of the visit to the dentist.

What are we to make of all this? Note that there does not appear to be any actual two-way communication between Croiset and the 'targets' in any of the above accounts. The targets had no idea that Croiset was accessing information about them. This differs entirely from mediumship where mediums make statements such as, 'He is telling me ... etc'. where there is a three-way communication between the medium, the sitter and the alleged communicator. However, Croiset does appear to tap in to the consciousness of the target person whether alive, dead, in the past or in the future. Curiouser and curiouser.

Now consider the statements that were made during experimentation. They were absolutely correct, and many of them were very specific and obscure – how can we explain that? The simple answer is that in our present model of reality we cannot. I think that you would at least agree that it was not just lucky guessing. In relation to the statements made by Croiset we would need to accurately know how many of the statements could be accepted by the other twenty-nine people in the room before it would be possible to calculate the actual probability of the results being due to chance, but the statements were so specific that the odds against chance would doubtless be enormous.

As I said earlier, this type of experiment was replicated over four hundred times by different experimenters from various countries, who achieved similar results. I leave you to digest that information. Whatever you think about all of this, there is no doubt that Gerard Croiset appeared to have an amazing psychic talent, if that's the correct term – he did not claim that he had any contact with a 'spirit world'. However, as already noted, his consciousness was in some way able to tap into other people who were alive or dead. Perhaps this is akin to some very precise form of remote viewing rather than straightforward mediumship? I do not know the answer.

I, personally, do not like the idea of precognition and retrocognition, but that is just too bad and I have to be sensible and follow where the evidence leads.

There are many misperceptions about mediumship. I would say that the standard definition of a medium is one who acts as an intermediary between the living and the dead, but, as we can see from Croiset, it may not be that simple.

Very little is clear-cut in these matters and it would be foolish to be dogmatic about any process. Perhaps precise definitions are not the way forward.

In 2018, the President of The Academy for Spiritual and Consciousness Studies, Mr James E. Beichler, Ph.D. offered the following opinion.

> I believe that we as individuals are subconsciously and constantly in contact with the universe as a whole and in its parts. This contact is the source of our intuition, paranormal phenomena and many other phenomena and events that cannot be explained by science. This worldview may seem a bit odd for me as a diehard physicist, but I am also a trained historian, which gives me a much broader view of science, how new ideas intermingle, evolve and grow to influence the human condition. Together these interests have driven me even deeper into studies of the human psyche, which has directly affected the physics in which I practice and conduct research.

I applaud his statement.

As far as continuation of consciousness is concerned, in my role as a psychical researcher, I try to look at these matters in as scientific a manner as possible but often the reality defies rationality. A few years ago I took an excellent medium to a case where a young couple were complaining about inexplicable noises in their house. In these types of cases I take a tape recorder with me. I drove Professor Archie Roy and the medium to the house. It was a fairly small, modern house with accommodation upstairs and downstairs. We sat downstairs and I began recording our conversations. We were told that they often heard quite definite footsteps coming from the bedroom that was directly above the lounge. By this time the medium had left the room as I had asked him to go upstairs and have a sense of anything that might be going on. He had not been given any information regarding the nature of the purported phenomena. He was quite happy with this and said that he would sit on the bed and 'tune in'. As I said, the rest of us were sitting downstairs when, after chatting for five to ten minutes, or thereabouts, we heard quite loud prolonged creaky footsteps coming from the bedroom above. There was no mistaking the source and they sounded as if they were going right across the middle of the ceiling of the lounge. I said, 'Oh the medium must have finished and is coming down'. He never appeared. I went upstairs to see what was happening to find him sitting on the edge of the bed, facing the door. I said, 'We heard you walking up and down, did you sense anything?' He looked puzzled and said, 'I haven't moved'. When I actually took time to look at the room I realised that he could not have walked up and down as the room could only hold a double bed. There was *no* place for him to walk! Unfortunately the tape recorder was an old one and did not clearly pick up the footsteps, but we all heard them clear as a bell. Due to the construction of the house there was no other property that could account for the source of the footsteps.

It appears to me that mediumship and consciousness cannot be separated. True mediumship requires a blending of the consciousness of the medium and that of another personality.

In mediumship a long prolonged message is not always necessary for an evidential reading. Very recently another respected medium known to me personally was asked to give a private reading to a man whose mother had just passed. The sitter was distraught and not coping well. The medium gave him excellent information about his mother, which did not seem to have much impact until the medium said, 'She wants to know why you are now sleeping on three pillows?'

The man's jaw visibly dropped and then he began to really listen. He had only used three pillows since her passing.

Another medium's private message was falling on stony ground until he said to the female recipient, 'Your son says you have to stop sleeping on his grave at night, it is far too cold and he is not there'. At this point the woman's husband, who was very dubious about the mediumistic process, was visibly flabbergasted as he responded by saying that no one knew of this except him and his wife. They then listened very carefully after that and received a great deal of help from that reading.

On a different vein, some people imagine that every 'message' given to a recipient at, for example, a public meeting would be one that was welcome. Not necessarily so. I attended a meeting a few years ago, and I cannot remember who the medium was, where a message was proffered to a woman, whom I knew, in the audience.

The medium said to her, 'I have your mother here'.

The response was less than enthusiastic. As I listened my heart sank, as I knew that she really disliked her mother.

The medium continued, 'She has come to offer you an apology'.

Little response – undaunted the medium continued, 'Will you accept an apology from her?'

After what seemed like a lifetime in deafening silence the woman replied, 'No'.

After a little hesitation the medium then described the recipient's last cat in great detail, and that was met with a lot more joy.

At another public meeting, a medium brought forward a gentleman to a lady in the audience and said, 'I have your husband here'.

The somewhat cynical response was, 'Oh yeah'.

Medium continued, 'He didn't come in to me in the usual way, he sort of slid in'.

Response, 'Oh that'll be him, he was a slippery sod'.

Undaunted the medium continued, 'He is bringing you a large bottle of champagne to acknowledge your recent birthday'.

Response, 'Oh he would, he liked his drink and you can tell him it's the best ****** birthday I have ever had now that he has gone!'

I have actually toned down the language in that exchange.

No love lost there then.

# 2

# Retrocognition

Seeing or knowing about things that happened in the past

There are many well-authenticated accounts of people who actually appear to have experienced events that happened years before, even from the dim and distant past.

Ancient battle sites are often locations where people report strange experiences.

The battle of Edgehill, 1642, has reportedly been "witnessed" by many people on various occasions through the years.

Even King Charles I was advised that local inhabitants had seen an apparition of this battle up to a year after it occurred. On hearing the reports he sent sceptical envoys to investigate. They returned considerably shaken since they had also witnessed the phenomenon. The battle scenes were not only re-enacted before their eyes but they were shocked when they actually recognised their former colleagues who had died there.

## *Mrs Dorothy Strong*

In 1960 Mrs Dorothy Strong was on holiday in Northumberland when she and her taxi driver were suddenly surrounded by a crowd of ragged soldiers. The soldiers appeared to be confused. On subsequent investigation by Mrs Strong it turned out that she and the taxi driver had unknowingly been on the site of the Battle of Otterburn, which had been fought in 1388.

## *Miss Smith*

In 1950 Miss Smith was journeying home from Brechin in her car accompanied by her small dog. Her car went into a ditch and she then had to walk home approximately eight miles along deserted farm roads. It was late at night.

As she approached the first houses in Letham village (Angus) she saw moving figures to her right bearing flaming torches, which made the dog growl. They were heading in the direction of Dunnichin Hill.

She carried on walking. To her right in a field about fifty yards away she saw more figures walking around what appeared to be a loch. (Mere)

The dog growled again – he appeared to be looking at the light from the torches.

By this time it was 2:00 a.m. and she became concerned that the dog would bark and awaken the people in the village.

She walked steadfastly on, finally leaving the lights and figures behind. It was only the next morning that the realisation of how strange the whole experience had been actually hit her.

She recollected that the figures were carrying long flaming torches in their left hands. It appeared that they were obviously looking for their own dead as they would bend down and turn a body over, and if it were not one that they wanted they would turn it back on its face.

Unknown to her she was on the site of the Battle of Nectanesmere, which took place in 685 AD. I find it interesting that the dog also appeared to see something and growled repeatedly.

The respected psychiatrist Dr James McHarg investigated this account and postulated the following possible explanations.

Hoax: although possible, was extremely unlikely due to the character and credibility of the witness.

Paramnesia: It was a false memory.

Cryptomnesia: Her mind contained subconscious hidden data, perhaps having previously read about the events that took place there. On questioning, she denied any prior knowledge of the events and had no knowledge of the *now vanished* loch.

Hallucination: Due to hidden knowledge along with the dark conditions and tiredness after walking for so long.

Retrocognition: she actually viewed the events as described, possibly due to a change in her consciousness leading to altered perception.

Retrocognition would be in line with Stone Tape Theory, which postulates that 'places and buildings' can retain or record some sort of memory of events that took place in that space. These events are usually, but not always, highly charged with emotion and at times it appears, as above, that people are in some way able to 'tune in' to view this psychic 'video'.

It is interesting to note that Miss Smith appeared to be more concerned about the possibility of her dog possibly barking and disturbing the residents than the spectacle in front of her.

We know that remote viewers and people such as Croiset can deliberately try to tap in to past events but sometimes, as illustrated in the examples above, these things also seem to occur spontaneously.

## *Mrs Buterbaugh*

Another less traumatic example of this phenomenon allegedly happened to Mrs Buterbaugh of the University of Nebraska.

American psychologist Gardner Murphy and psychiatrist Herbert L. Klemme reported a case of ostensible retrocognition involving Mrs. Coleen Buterbaugh, a secretary at Nebraska Wesleyan University, Lincoln, Nebraska. Mrs. Buterbaugh's experience occurred on October 3, 1963 when she was asked by Dean Sam Dahl to deliver a message to a colleague, Professor Martin, at his office suite in the C.C. White Building nearby. As she entered the building and walked along its large hall she heard the sounds of students playing music in some rooms reserved for music practice. In particular she heard a marimba being played. Entering the first suite she stopped after a few steps because she experienced a strong smell, a musty unpleasant odour. She glanced up and saw the figure of a very tall black-haired woman in a shirtwaist top and ankle-length skirt. This woman was reaching out with her right arm towards the upper right hand shelf of an old music cabinet, which contained scripts of choral music. Mrs. Buterbaugh described it thus:

> As I first walked into the room everything was quite normal. I was about four steps into the room when the strong odour hit me. When I say strong odour, I mean the kind that simply stops you in your tracks and almost chokes you. I was looking down at the floor, as one often does when walking, and as soon as that odour stopped me I felt that there was someone in the room with me. It was then that I was aware that there were no noises out in the hall. Everything was deathly quiet. I looked up and something drew my eyes to the cabinet along the wall in the next room. I looked up and there she was. She had her back to me, reaching up into one of the shelves of the cabinet with her right hand, and standing perfectly still. She never moved. She was not transparent, and yet I knew she wasn't real. While I was looking at her she just faded away – not parts of her body one at a time, but her whole body all at once.
>
> Up until the time she faded away, I was not aware of anyone else being in the suite of rooms, but just about the time of her fading out I felt as though I still was not alone. To my left was a desk and I had a feeling there was a man sitting at that desk. I turned around and saw no one, but still felt his presence. When that feeling of his presence left I have no idea because it was then, when I looked out the window behind that desk, that I got frightened and left the room. I am not sure whether I ran or walked out of the room. When I looked out that window there wasn't one modern thing out there. The street, Madison Street, which is less than a half block away from the building, was not even there and neither was the new Willard House. That was when I realised that these people were not in my time, but that I was back in their time.
>
> It was not until I was back out in the hall that I again heard the familiar noises. This must have all taken place in a few seconds because the girls that were going into the orientation class as I entered the rooms were still going in and someone was still playing the marimba.

Shaken by her experience, Mrs. Buterbaugh returned to her office in the old Main Building. She tried to continue typing but was so upset that she kept breaking off. Finally she went to Dean Dahl and told him of the strange event. In later discussions it was suggested that there could have been some resemblance between the tall black-haired woman Mrs. Buterbaugh had seen in the office and a Miss Clarissa U. Mills, a lecturer in theory and piano, who had used that office many years before and who had died suddenly in 1936 in a room just across the hall. In some old yearbooks, never before seen by Mrs. Buterbaugh, a picture of Miss Mills was subsequently found. The figure that she saw in that room had been standing with her back towards Mrs. Buterbaugh so that the face was hidden but in many particulars the figure resembled Miss Mills who had been a very tall, thin, black-haired spinster interested in music and choral group singing. Indeed the filing cabinet, before which the apparition had stood, actually contained choral group arrangements, some of which dated back to a time before Miss Mills' death. In addition, the bushy, bouffant hairstyle and clothes of the apparition were consistent with the fashions of 1915. Miss Mills had started work at the college in 1912 and in the picture of her discovered in the old yearbooks she wore such a hairstyle.

Mrs. Buterbaugh was further able to describe what she saw when she looked out of the window behind the desk, where she had had a feeling of a man's presence:

> The window was open. Even though it was fairly early in the morning, it appeared as though it was a very warm summer afternoon. It was very still. There were a few scattered trees – about two on my right (east) and about three on my left (west). It seems to me there were more, but these are the only ones I can be definite about. The rest was open field; the new Willard sorority house and also Madison Street were not there. I remember seeing a very vague outline of some sort of building to my right and that is about all. There was nothing else but open field.

A careful investigation followed, including a complete psychiatric and neurological examination of Mrs. Buterbaugh who seemed to be a happily married woman with four children in good mental health who worked efficiently as secretary to the Dean.

You may remember that Dean Dahl had sent Mrs Buterbaugh to that room with a written message to give to Professor Martin but the message was actually to be given to a visiting music professor from Scotland who was at that time was busy arranging choral group singing.

Back in 1936 Miss Mills had died in the office across the hall shortly before 9:00 a.m. having struggled through the bitter wind to get to the C.C. White Building. Mrs. Buterbaugh also arrived at the same building shortly before 9:00 a.m.

Whether there was any significance in Miss Mills' being at the cabinet containing choral music scripts and the Scottish professor's arranging choral group singing, we can't know but it's interesting to note.

It had been suspected that the strange smell experienced by Mrs. Buterbaugh could have been the 'aura' that certain people have as a warning before having a fit. This suspicion was one of the reasons that Mrs. Buterbaugh was persuaded to undergo a medical examination. But as Gardner Murphy said at the time: 'It is quite likely that it was a symbol or marker of a transition at that moment from her normal state to an altered state of consciousness in which she became capable of experiencing her ostensible retrocognition'.

It transpired that Mrs. Buterbaugh was a good hypnotic subject. She was regressed under deep hypnosis to the 'time' of her experience; she recounted it and her account did not differ from her previous statements.

So, here we have a case of another perfectly well balanced woman, both physically and psychologically, catching a glimpse of an event in the past. There are many such cases.

In all of these cases there was no interaction with the people of the past, they did not appear to see the percipients and yet the percipients could perceive them, as could a dog. Some would posit the idea that the scenes and beings observed in these cases are a sort of holographic image. Mrs Butterbaugh said that she 'sensed' the presence of a man in the room – I wonder – can you sense the presence of a holographic image? I ask the question but offer no answer or opinion.

Now let us move from the past to the future.

# 3

# Precognition

'Knowing' about things that happen in the future

Most of us assume that time is linear only moving forwards but time is a man made concept.

No one really knows the nature of time. Current scientific wisdom suggests that time bends in relationship to space.

It is known that space itself can be 'dented' by mass; perhaps some similar principle may cause time to be altered by space. The Concise Oxford English Dictionary definition of time is 'Duration, continued existence, progress of things viewed as affecting persons or things'. This does not seem very helpful, although it is interesting to me that it takes note of human experience in trying to formulate a definition.

There is a growing acknowledgement among physicists, including several Nobel laureates that the universe (or universes) may exist in higher dimensional space. Superstring theory predicts that the number of dimensions is ten. At the time of writing, the latest Multiverse theory that I have heard about predicts up to eleven dimensions. Neither of these theories has been empirically demonstrated.

Because of this multi-dimensional aspect, precognition may be knowledge or experience of a *possible* future; it may not be written in stone. I am reminded of the film *Sliding Doors* where they illustrated that a decision a person makes one day can affect the next step in their pathway of life. It could be something as simple as choosing to turn left instead of right at the end of a road that may change their future forever. Precognitive events appear to take place in various levels of consciousness, including a dream or waking state.

## *Jeane Dixon*

Jeane Dixon was an American psychic who, as a child, appeared to be able to predict future events. When Jeane was eight, a gypsy gave her a crystal, which she subsequently used to help her to concentrate while she was actually seeking to predict the future, although her predictions normally came to her in times of silence or meditation.

It is well attested that she accurately foretold the time of deaths of John F. Kennedy, Robert Kennedy, Martin Luther King, Ghandi and Marilyn Munroe. More details about this will be given later.

She claimed that her predictions fell into two groups: revelation and perceptions.

Revelations: which she stated are the visions of the unavoidable events that shape the world's destiny and therefore cannot be changed.

Perceptions: which foreshadow future happenings and do not *have* to take place. In other words they can be altered by a change in behaviour by the perceiver or some other life changing action.

Her revelations were few in number, which we might expect since they deal with large-scale events that are seldom intended for one individual.

In 1946 she forecast, to the very day, that there would be an announcement on Feb 20$^{th}$ 1947 about the partitioning of India. At the time an Indian diplomat based in Washington openly scoffed at her prediction.

On the morning of the appointed day he telephoned her to tease her about the unfulfilled prophecy. Her reply was that, 'The day was not over' and sure enough, the next morning the papers carried the story that India was being partitioned.

Two of the most high profile murders in the twentieth century were the murders of US President John F. Kennedy and his brother Robert Kennedy. The charisma of the Kennedy brothers and the hopes laid upon them by the American people, and many around the world produced a deep sense of shock and despair when John F. Kennedy was shot and killed in Dallas in November 1963 and followed by the murder of Robert Kennedy in June 1968.

Jeane Dixon, in an article in *Parade* magazine in the issue of May 13, 1956 was described as *Washington's Incredible Crystal-gazer.* Politicians and celebrities listened to her and she had acquired a reputation as a seer by making a number of prophecies that appeared to hit the mark.

She is alleged to have told Franklin D. Roosevelt that he would be elected as president for four terms of office. It is reported that when in November 1944 he asked her how long he had to live she replied, 'Six months or less'. He must have been thrilled about that. She also told him, 'China will go Communist and become our greatest trouble. Africa will be our next biggest worry in the foreign field'.

During World War II she allegedly told Harry S. Truman that he would become President of the United States and would serve for two terms. By these and other prophecies Jeane Dixon had achieved her very credible reputation when the next statements in *Parade* appeared. The following passage appeared in the May, 1956 issue.

> As for the 1960 election, Mrs Dixon thinks it will be dominated by labor and won by a Democrat. But he will be assassinated or die in office, though not necessarily in his first term.

Although this is not a complete description of the circumstances surrounding the murder of President Kennedy it is none the less a remarkable statement. She prophesied categorically that the man who would be elected in 1960 would be a Democrat and he would die in office or be assassinated within the eight years of being elected. Her prediction, made over seven years before President Kennedy's assassination in 1963 was absolutely true.

W.H.W. Sabine raises an interesting question with regard to this prophecy and other events associated with it. Writing in the *Journal of the American Society for Psychical Research* he asked:

> Could the publication [in *Parade*] have contributed to cause the event? When an event depends upon human activities, and when publication has taken place a considerable time before fulfilment, causation by the percipient is obviously one of the possible explanations of an apparent precognition. *Parade* was circulated in New Orleans where, at the date in question, Lee Harvey

> Oswald, Kennedy's assassin was living as a youth of sixteen. If Oswald saw the article, and the reference in it to the Kremlin shakeup it might attract the attention of a young Marxist – the idea of the assassination of a future President could thus have entered his mind. In any case, it is evident that the idea of such an assassination, and even a measure of expectation of it, was thus implanted in numerous minds all over the country; while in Washington Mrs. Dixon, according to Mrs. Montgomery (her biographer), was constantly reiterating her warning. Thus it may not be necessary to suggest even a telepathic influence in theorizing that Mrs. Dixon's widely known prophecy could have been causative in the events leading to the assassination.

That is indeed a possible suggestion but my own opinion of that idea is that it is a stretch too far in 'What if'.

However, Sabine's argument has to be taken somewhat seriously as a possible explanation for what many would believe is one of the most impressive prophecies of modern times. The self-fulfilling prophecy has been with us for a very long time in many forms. If the shaman of a savage tribe tells them that to go to war against the tribe over the hill it will result in victory or defeat, the warriors, knowing of the prophecy, will undoubtedly fight better or worse according to their expectations, thus helping to bring about the result predicted. If a number of people conspire to tell a man at various times in the morning that they dreamed that he would have a particularly bad day, it is quite likely that he will be so upset psychologically that he will make mistakes guaranteed to give him a bad day or at least affect him psychosomatically. In any country with its fair share of potential assassins, the reiterated warning that a particular public figure is in danger could just possibly trigger the attempt.

Nonetheless, if this is the explanation, and the corollary is that Mrs. Dixon's premonition about J.F.K. was the cause and not effect, it is difficult to explain certain other aspects of the affair. According to Charles Neilson Gattey, in October 1963 she told the psychiatrist Dr F. R. Riesemann and the journalist Ruth Montgomery of a vision in which the vice-presidential plaque was removed from Lyndon Johnson's door. She said that the man responsible for doing this had a two-syllable name with five or six letters, the second letter being definitely an 's', The first looking like an 'O' and the last ending with a little curve that went straight up. This certainly fits the name 'Oswald'. Again, as November

1963 began, Dixon evidently told various people in Washington that her feeling regarding the President's danger to his life was getting stronger. On the week of the murder, she is alleged to have seen on Tuesday a vision of John F. Kennedy being shot in the head while on the Friday at breakfast she said, 'This is the day it will happen'.

The inability to obtain clearly the name of his assassin is reminiscent of that annoying everyday happening when we seek to recall a name and cannot get it, though tantalisingly we perceive a fair impression of its length and shape. One or two names similar to the desired name may come up before the sought for name surfaces. In addition, the growing unease driving Mrs. Dixon to tell people is quite in line with what we know about the effect that premonitions have on people; this is what a Dr Barker called the *Pre-disaster Syndrome.*

Seers are part of the history of nearly every nation and cult. Scottish Highland second sight is very well known, the most famous prophet being the Brahan Seer; time after time his predictions have come true.

One statement made by him 150 years before the building of the Caledonian Canal was, "Strange as it may seem to you this day the time will come, and it's not far off, when full rigged ships will be seen sailing eastward and westward by the back of Tomnahurich". This turned out to be perfectly correct. Although he died over 300 years ago some of his prophecies are still pending.

In 1967 The British Premonitions Bureau was set up. In 1968 The Central Premonitions Registry was founded in New York. The British Bureau closed in 1977

Although many claims were submitted to these agencies there were few direct hits.

It was, however, noted that sometimes a premonition comes to a person who is ostensibly not directly involved with it. As an example, on June 22, 1922, Field Marshal Sir Henry Wilson was shot by Irish terrorists in London.

## *Lady Londonderry*

A casual friend of the Field Marshal, Lady Londonderry, had dreamed of his murder ten days earlier. She saw him shot by two men in front of a cottage on a moor. The following day she told two people about her dream. When the assassination took place Lady Londonderry found that every detail of the event corresponded with those in her dream with one notable exception. Whereas she saw the murder taking place outside a cottage, it took place in the street outside a London house. None the less all other details were correct.

It seems logical to suggest, by the laws of probability alone, that if enough predictions are logged then by chance some of them must come true. However, I don't feel that this depressing outlook covers the exact nature of many predictions such as the 1912 sinking of the *Titanic*, the avoidable tragedy of the airship R101 in 1930 and the 1966 Aberfan disaster. So let us now consider the many well-authenticated predictions about these particular events.

## *Titanic*

The sinking of the liner *Titanic* in April 1912 was an event that created in many harrowing emotions of loss, horror, agony and shock. This great liner, the largest ship in the world and the pride of British shipbuilding was widely believed to be unsinkable.

On the April 10, *Titanic* set sail on her maiden voyage. On board were passengers who included all social classes from millionaires and their entourage, servants and poor immigrant families seeking a new life in the USA and Canada. En route, Captain Edward Smith, undoubtedly feeling bullish and believing in the invincibility of his ship, ignored five warnings about icebergs in the north Atlantic. RMS *Titanic* was steaming at full speed during the night of April 14, when at 11: 40 p.m. it struck an iceberg which ripped the ship's hull below the waterline as easily as a tin-opener can open a can. A fatal flaw in the design of the watertight bulkheads, highlighted by the flooding of the five damaged bow compartments, allowed the icy waters to spill over into successive sections thus sealing the great liner's fate. Nearly three hours after the collision the ship sank. During the ordeal many passengers were so convinced that the ship was unsinkable they refused to leave it and this unshakable refusal to board the lifeboats undoubtedly increased the loss of life. Of the 2,223 passengers and crew aboard, only 703 survived.

The high number of fatalities was mainly due to the fact that the liner carried too few lifeboats and many of those lifeboats were not full to capacity when they left the sinking ship. Those left to jump or fall into the water perished mostly due to exposure to the icy waters of the north Atlantic where it is reckoned that even for a strong swimmer death would result within fifteen minutes. A horrendous scenario.

Professor Ian Stevenson, a psychiatrist at the University of Virginia, collected a number of paranormal phenomena accounts connected with the sinking of the *Titanic,* and suggested that such disasters may produce some kind of 'psychic shock' in the world, by some means unknown to us, due to their very unexpectedness. He speculated that the sinking of the *Titanic* might have generated an emotional shock not present in disasters that are less unexpected such as the wartime sinking of the Lusitania and most military battles.

Of the nineteen cases collected by Stevenson, ten were ostensibly precognitive. One of them, at first glance, apparently demonstrates a remarkable foreknowledge of many of the details of the sinking and of the ship. Morgan Robertson, in 1898, fourteen years before the *Titanic* tragedy wrote a novel called *Futility* in which he described a liner named the *Titan.* On a voyage in April, it struck an iceberg and sank. Like *Titanic, Titan* was believed to be unsinkable because it had watertight compartments. It also carried too few lifeboats; therefore the sinking resulted in large loss of life.

Stevenson compared the statistics of the fictional *Titan* with *Titanic.*

| | *Titan* | *Titanic* |
|---|---|---|
| Number of persons aboard: | 3,000 | 2,207 |
| Number of lifeboats: | 24 | 20 |
| Speed at impact: (in knots) | 25 | 23 |
| Displacement tonnage: | 75,000 | 66,000 |
| Length of the liner: (in feet) | 800 | 882.5 |
| Number of propellers: | 3 | 3 |

Stevenson noted that the correspondence is either exact or impressive on ten points: name of ship; myth of unsinkability; collision with iceberg; sinking in month of April; displacement tonnage; length of ship; speed of ship at impact; number of propellers; number of lifeboats and the loss of life.

It is also interesting to note that contrary to popular belief, the *Titanic* by no means had a full complement of passengers on its one and only voyage – it was only about two-thirds full.

Professor Stevenson, while admitting that the similarities between Robertson's *Titan* and *Titanic* may suggest a premonition pointed out that inference could be an adequate source of Robertson's story. Inference may, from knowledge of the factors forming a situation and knowledge of trends, enable a future development to be forecast without involving any paranormal faculty. He wrote,

> A writer of the 1890s familiar with man's repeated hubris might reasonably infer that he would overreach himself in the construction of ocean liners which then, with skyscrapers and airplanes just beginning, were man's greatest engineering marvels. Granting then a penetrating awareness of man's growing and excessive confidence in marine engineering, a thoughtful person might make additional inferences about the details of the tragedy to come. A large ship would probably have great power and speed; the name Titan has connoted power and security for several thousand years; overconfidence would neglect the importance of lifeboats; recklessness would race the ship through the areas of the Atlantic icebergs; these drift south in the spring, making April a likely month for collision.

Personally I think that this is again stretching the 'what if' scenario too far, there are far too many specific details.

Nevertheless, even if Morgan Robertson's 1898 novel is to be explained as a very remarkable use of inference, it is impossible to attribute this to some of the other cases of ostensible precognition about this disaster. Here are some examples.

On March 23, 1912, Mr. J.C. Middleton booked passage on the *Titanic.* Some ten days before the sailing date he had a dream which he related at a later time. 'I saw her [the *Titanic*] floating on the sea, keel upwards and her passengers and crew swimming around her'. The dream was repeated the following night. Mr. Middleton, although feeling uneasy, depressed, and despondent by his dreams, did not cancel his trip until four days later after receiving a cable from New York telling him that for business reasons he should postpone it for a few days. It was then that he told members of his family and his friends about his dreams, prior to the ship's sailing. Confirmation was given by two people whom he told and their reports were published in the Proceedings of the Society for Psychical Research)

Joan Grant, in her autobiography *Far Memory* relates how her parents, Mr. & Mrs. Jack Marshall, stood on the roof of their home with their family on April 10th, 1912. The house overlooked the Solent opposite the Isle of Wight. As they watched the *Titanic* move down the Solent on its maiden voyage, Mrs. Marshall became agitated. She clutched her husband's arm and cried out, 'That ship is going to sink before she reaches America'. There was nothing that anyone present could do to calm her. When told that the ship was unsinkable she shouted, 'Don't stand there staring at me! Do something! You fools, I can see hundreds of people struggling in the icy water! Are you all so blind that you are going to let them drown?'

Joan Grant, who as a child witnessed this scene, wrote:

> During the next few days everyone was careful not to mention the *Titanic* but her mother was nervy and father looked harassed. It must have been almost a relief for her when everyone knew that the *Titanic* had struck an iceberg: not nearly so lonely for her as waiting until it happened.

In 1912 Mr. V.N. Turvey, a sensitive, predicted on Wednesday, April 10, that 'A great liner will be lost'. On Saturday, April 12, he sent this prediction in a letter to a Madame I. de Steiger, adding that the liner would be lost in two days. Madame de Steiger received this letter a few hours after the *Titanic* sank.

Professor Stevenson also gathered together a number of precognitions that were associated with William Stead, the crusading journalist and editor who was also an advocate of Spiritualism. Stead was a passenger on the *Titanic* and he went down with it.

Some years before he died, Stead himself seemed to have been preoccupied by the theme of disaster at sea. As editor of the *Pall Mall Gazette*, in the 1880s he published a fictional article, a survivor's tale of the sinking of a great liner. Stead added an editorial note; 'This is exactly what might take place, and what will take place, if liners are sent to sea short of lifeboats'.

In 1892, Stead returned to this theme, publishing an article in the *Review of Reviews* concerning a liner sinking as a result of a collision with an iceberg. Its sole surviving passenger is rescued by the White Star liner, the *Majestic*, a remarkable coincidence in itself since at that time the captain of the Majestic was Captain Edward Smith, who became captain of the *Titanic* and went down with his ship. Stead also described a vision he had of himself dying by violence as one of many in a throng while in 1909 he gave a lecture to the Cosmos Club in which he pictured himself as shipwrecked and calling for help.

Stead consulted sensitives from time to time including Cheiro the palmist, and Mr. W. de Kerlor. On June 21, 1911, Cheiro wrote to Stead telling him, among other things, that:

> … from your date of birth in the Sign of Cancer, otherwise known as the First House of Water, in my humble opinion, any danger of violent death to you must be by water and nothing else. Very critical and dangerous for you should be April, 1912, especially about the middle of the month. So don't travel by water then if you can help it. If you do, you will be liable to meet with such danger to your life that the very worst may happen! I know I am not wrong about this "water" danger; I only hope I am correct, or at least that you won't be travelling somewhere about that time.

The second sensitive, Mr. de Kerlor, told Stead that he would go to America. At that time Stead had no plans to do so. The sensitive said:

> I can see a picture of a huge black ship, of which I see the back portion; where the name of the ship should be written there is a wreath of immortelles … I can only see half of the ship: that symbol may mean by the time this ship will be completed, when one will be able to see it in its whole length, it is perhaps then that you will go on your journey.

Later, the same sensitive had a dream, which he applied to Stead. He told Stead that he had, dreamt that:

> I was in the midst of a catastrophe on the water; there were masses (more than a thousand) of bodies struggling in the water and I was among them. I would hear their cries for help.

He warned Stead that the black ship 'meant limitations, difficulties and death'.

In spite of these warnings Stead took the trip on the *Titanic* and did in fact go down with her.

As a spiritualist you would have thought that he would have known better!

Professor Stevenson was sent the following account of an experience by Mrs. Charles Hughes of 19a Shelton Old Road, Stoke-on-Trent, England:

The most vivid dream I ever had was when I was fourteen. I was sleeping with my grandmother who lived next door to us. I was on the main road at Hanford, which was then Trentham Road and now it's Stone Road, when suddenly I saw a very large ship a short distance away as if in Trentham Park. I saw figures walking about on it, and I just stood wondering what it was doing there and then suddenly it lowered at one end and I heard a terrific scream. I must have wakened up making a noise because it frightened Gran. She said, "No more suppers for you, lady; dreams are a pack of daft," after I had told her what I'd seen.

After a while I must have gone to sleep again and saw the very same scene and when the people screamed I must have done. Gran was real livid with me this time and said I wasn't stopping with her again at night.

This all happened on the Friday night, April 12, 1912. The next morning I told my mother and I was really very upset at what I'd seen and what Gran had said.

Now Grandma kept a shop and there was a man who came in every morning early for tobacco as he fetched fish from Stoke Station. On the Monday morning, April 15, after my dream he came in and opened a morning paper, the *Daily Mirror*, and he said, "Hey, old woman, is this your son?" and being as she could not read and her sight was not too good she asked me to look. There was a picture of the crew serving on the *Titanic* on the middle page. I read a little bit and then I stopped. I saw the picture of my uncle, Grandma's son, my mother's brother.

I asked the man to stop in with Gran while I took the paper next door to Mom. She looked and said, "Oh, your dream". Mother broke the news to her that her son, Mrs. Hughes' uncle, had been drowned, a scene I'll never forget. Uncle was the Fourth Senior Engineer and was due for retirement after this trip. He had served on the HMS *Hawke* and the S.S. *Celtic* and was transferred to the *Titanic*.

Stevenson adds that he later visited Mrs. Hughes and she gave him additional information about the experience. Unfortunately, both her mother and grandmother had died by then. Mrs. Hughes told Professor Stevenson that both her dreams were vivid, possessing a strong emotional intensity. She confirmed that the uncle, a Mr. Leonard Hodgkinson, was the son of Mrs. Hughes' grandmother with whom she used to stay at nights. He was Mrs. Hughes' mother's brother who was due to retire and since he had an ambition to sail on all the White Star liners he transferred to the Titanic for her maiden voyage. It was a late decision and so, while his wife knew he was on the Titanic, his mother, sister, niece (the percipient) and other members of the family did not.

It was speculated that the location of the 'very large ship' in Trentham Park in Mrs. Hughes' dreams might be partly due to the facts that the park was familiar to her and it possessed a large lake with facilities for boating. Nevertheless, another park at Hanley was closer and she also frequented it as a child, so the jury could be out on that idea.

A further ostensible precognitive experience was sent to Professor Stevenson by Mrs. North K. Mathews:

> I was about eleven years of age when I first heard that my mother, Mrs. Mary Keziah Roberts, was going to sail on the great new ship called the *Titanic*. I was a very reserved and quiet child, but very deeply impressed. I looked at my dear mother, who was gaily combing her hair. She was looking at me in the looking glass for a few minutes and I looked at her and she smiled and threw her head back and sang; she had a sweet musical voice too. She sang, 'Yip-i-addie-i -aye ... I don't care what becomes of me ... lah, lah, lah'. Then I turned to her and said quietly, "Mama, why do you sing like that?" I felt sad and could not say very much. I said again, "I don't want you to sing that song again; I don't want you to sail on the *Titanic*". With this she stopped combing her lovely long hair, and stopped singing and stopped laughing too. After a few minutes she said to me whilst still looking into the looking glass at me,
>
> 'Oh Tabby, Tabby, I must tell your father about that'. She was going to sing again then just went on combing her hair and I looked through the window quietly, with a strange sense of doom. Certainly no elation. We were living at No.9 Chestnut Grove, West Bridgeford, Nottingham, at the time. My father, David Roberts, became quite impressed at what I had said, as I was nine years of age when I first had most powerful and correct impressions.
>
> Mrs. Mathews confirmed to Professor Stevenson that she thought that something was going to happen, 'Both to my mother and also to the fine new boat she was going shortly to sail in'.

The inevitable happened to the *Titanic*, but happily Mrs Roberts was one of the survivors.

In another example, Professor Stevenson learned through a newspaper obituary that a Mr. Colin Macdonald had refused to join the *Titanic*'s crew because of an impression he had of disaster for the ship. Mr. Macdonald's daughter when interviewed by Professor Stevenson showed him a newspaper account of a relevant interview her father had given four years previously. Mrs. Fernsworth, Mr. Macdonald's daughter, said that her father had corrected a mistake in the newspaper account and that it then agreed with his memory of the experience which he had often narrated to his family.

In 1912 Mr. Macdonald, a thirty-three year old marine engineer, was offered the position of second engineer on the Titanic. Although this would have meant an important promotion for him Mr. MacDonald had such an uneasy feeling that he should not sail on the Titanic that he refused the offer three times. That proved to be a wise decision as the man who finally took his place, Mr. J. Hesketh, died in the disaster.

We can see from these examples that premonitions appear to come in various ways and with different strengths of emotions, almost from 'just a feeling' to a deep down feeling of dread.

Although these examples are a very small cross section of those reported it does demonstrate that there have been a number of premonitions about the sinking of the *Titanic*.

In 1970 Professor Ian Stevenson published a paper on 'Precognition of disasters' in the *Journal of the American Society for Psychical Research*, 64(2), 187-210, in which he highlighted the strengths and weaknesses in the examples of premonitions associated with the *Titanic* tragedy.

## *R101*

In my book, *More Things you Can do When You're Dead* I described some amazing post mortem mediumistic communications, which provided compelling evidence for survival of consciousness after death, regarding the members of the deceased crew of the airship R101, which crashed in France on October 5, 1930 killing 48 of the 54 passengers and crew.

There were a number of reported premonitions associated with the R101 tragedy. Perhaps a forthcoming disaster produces Barker's 'Pre-disaster syndrome', which a sensitive person can pick up on. No one really knows.

In 1924 the British government decided to order the construction of two giant airships. One was built by government employees at the Royal Airship Works, Cardington. The other was constructed by a private firm, which was a subsidiary of the aircraft company, Vickers. The vision behind the enterprise was of powerful airships flying the long routes of the British Empire, bringing prestige to the United Kingdom and thus removing the monopoly which the Germans had on airship flight at the time.

By September 1930 the Vickers airship named R100, had passed her trials and had crossed the Atlantic and returned to the UK. It was a success. Meanwhile, work continued on the government's 'baby' the R101.

In every aspect, the R101 was an outstanding example of how not to build an airship. The planned lift of sixty tons was found to be 35 tons when the ship was completed. The fuel weight reduced this to ten tons and by the time crew, ballast, spare parts, etc. were added, the lift had practically disappeared. The framework was too heavy, the engines were massively heavy diesels, the bags were overinflated and the chafing of these against a multitude of rivets was quickly wearing innumerable holes in them.

By June 1930, the R101, in a seeming act of desperation, had been cut in two and extended by inserting a new middle section. More adjustments were made, including cabins being removed and parachutes being removed in an effort to lighten the load wherever possible.

Subsequently, during the few remaining hours of testing, it became even more obvious that the R101 still had serious problems. The Air Minister, Lord Thomson, however, had an overriding problem of his own. He had planned that the maiden flight should take him to Karachi to participate in a British Empire conference before flying him back to the UK. It is possible that to a Government minister the contemplation of his triumphant descent from the skies, so to speak, in the giant airship, played a large part in his insistence that the flight should be made as scheduled. His will prevailed against every reasonable opinion.

At 6:36 p.m. on October 4 1930, the R1ol left its mast at Cardington and staggered on its way. Yawing and pitching, never achieving a height much greater than its own length, it managed by night-time to reach Beauvais in France, There disaster struck; the hull and bags were ruptured, the 5.5 million cubic feet of hydrogen ignited and the R101, with most of its crew and passengers, perished in the resulting fire. Only six people survived. Among the dead was the Air Minister himself, the

Director of Civil Aviation and Flight Lieutenant R. Carmichael Irwin, the ship's captain.

The end of the sister-ship, the Rloo, was ignominious. Although successful, the Government decreed that it be scrapped because of the dreadful fate of the R101.

Did the tragic and unexpected end of the R1ol produce any well-attested cases of ostensible precognition in the manner similar to that of the *Titanic* disaster? Well, yes indeed.

In Dame Edith Lyttelton's book *Some Cases of Prediction* we find two such cases. On February 24, 1934 she received the following letter.

> 100 Woodcroft Road,
> Liverpool
> 23.2.34
>
> Madam,
>
> I listened with greatest interest to your talk this evening upon the subject of 'Premonition and Prevision' and have not the least doubt that these two particular things play an enormous part in our lives. With regard to your request, I can mention a very remarkable happening, under the term 'Prevision'.
>
> On two occasions, weeks before the ill-fated disaster to the British Airship R1ol at Beauvais – I dreamed of this terrible happening. The clarity of vision was astounding; every detail could be seen.
>
> I saw the huge ship plunge in flames, followed by a terrific explosion, almost frightening. Strange enough, the dream was repeated about a week after.
>
> As you stated tonight so few would have believed me, that I revealed my experiences to one person, a particular friend of mine, who is a keen psychic. He agreed entirely with me, as he also thought it was doomed.
>
> To me it was a most impressive happening, and was almost clear enough the following morning to sketch.
>
> I am submitting this letter in all sincerity as I feel, and believe, that Premonition and Prevision, are something very real, and transcend far above the human plane of thought.
>
> Faithfully yours,
> J.S. Wright.

Dame Edith wrote Mr. Wright seeking corroboration and the date of the dreams. Mr. Wright replied that he could not give the exact date of either dream, but his friend Mr. Coxon would corroborate his statement. Mr. Coxon, as promised, sent Dame Edith the corroboration sought for.

25 Brierfield Road,<br>
Liverpool, 15<br>
10.3.36

Dear Madam,

It has afforded me much interest to read the letter you have written to my friend Mr. J. Wright, 100 Woodcroft Road of this city. You are asking for my confirmation that Mr. Wright's dream was well previous to the loss of the R.101. May I assure you that at least six months prior to the disaster we had interchanged frequently on the vision, so much so, that on several occasions we had been on the point of communicating with the War Office.

Knowing however, from past experience, how futile it has been to make any impression on this Governmental Department, we refrained from pressing the matter.

Both Mr Wright and myself were fully convinced the R101 was doomed. Trusting this letter has been of some little assistance.

Yours truly,<br>
G. Coxon.

The second last paragraph of Mr. Coxon's letter is ironically apt, remembering how adamant the Air Minister Lord Thomson had been in insisting in the face of severe criticism that the flight of the R.1ol should go on as planned.

The second case was sent to Dame Edith by Mr. R.W. Boyd.

125 Wellington Road,<br>
Bush Hill Park,<br>
Enfield<br>
7.3.34

Dear Madam,

Having read your talk on the subject of 'Premonition and Prevision' in *The Listener*, my interest has been aroused and in response to your invitation I hope that the following dream experience may be of interest.

On October 3rd in 1930 I dreamed that I saw a large airship crash. After some preliminary difficulties in manoeuvring it landed on to the top of a hill and burst into flames. Many people were silhouetted against the bright yellow flames and were trying to escape, but none succeeded so far as I am able to remember.

The fact that the crash occurred on the top of a hill was very much impressed upon me as I was very excited and dashed about from place to place but was unable to help anybody. Further details of the dream I am not able to remember clearly.

I awoke the next morning with my mind very full of what had happened in the dream and the very first thing I did was to see if the morning newspapers had any news of an airship disaster, with the airship R101 in mind as this was just preparing for her flight to India. There was no account of any disaster and I decided that the dream was nothing more than a dream.

But on Sunday morning, October 6th, I learned with curious feeling that R101 had crashed at Beauvais, less than 48 hours after my dream. You will probably be interested to learn that I related the dream to at least one person, my fiancée, between October 3rd and October 5th and she can corroborate the facts I have set out.

When later, photographs appeared in the newspapers and newsreel films were shown, an officer on horseback was a prominent figure amongst those present and of course it is common knowledge that R1ol crashed into a hill after losing height through the effects of rain.

I hope this account may be of interest and use to you.

Yours sincerely,

R.W. Boyd

Again Dame Edith sought corroboration. In reply to her letter, Mr. Boyd's fiancée wrote:

55 Gardenia Road,
Bush Hill Park,
Enfield
19th September 1934

Dear Madam,

I trust you will forgive my neglect in not writing to you as promised for so long, and believe me that it is not through lack of interest. I very much appreciate your study and feel sorry that I have not helped you by an earlier reply.

The following is my fiancé's dream as far as I am able to recollect. He related it to me the day after he had dreamed, and to my mind the significance of it is marked by reason of the events, which followed three days afterwards, namely the disaster of the airship R101.

He was standing at the foot of a high hill over which the sun appeared to be setting. There came into view an airship, which, as it neared the hill, seemed to break into two pieces and was suddenly in flames. So vivid was it that he could discern the burning bodies of the people as they fell from the plane. He was conscious of policemen clothed in French uniform who arrived on horseback to help. He himself was powerless to assist as he felt as though he was watching apart. His own words were 'Like a disembodied spirit'. The dream was emphasised by the fact that when we visited a cinema the following week and saw a film of the R101 disaster, my fiancé was amazed to realise that the scene was almost identical with that of his dream, especially in the appearance of the French gendarmes who were shown examining the debris.

I find this all particularly remarkable, in so much that he is not a person who dreams often, and is usually quite unaffected by the small events which we are apt to call coincidence.

I must again apologise for the late arrival of this letter and I hope very much that it will be of use to you.

Yours sincerely,
Catherine Hare.

Dame Edith's opinion, to which most people subscribed, was that the details in Mr. Boyd's dream were too exact to be due to chance.

## *Aberfan*

I now cite a rather different example, and one much more recent. I will, provide you with examples from the collection of ostensible premonitions of the Aberfan disaster compiled by the late Dr. J. C. Barker.

At approximately 9:15 a.m. on October 21, 1966, a huge coal tip, rendered unstable by underground water, slid down a mountainside in Wales, United Kingdom on to the little mining village of Aberfan. The avalanche of black slurry killed one hundred and forty four people of which one hundred and twenty eight were schoolchildren. They were mainly from the Pantglas Junior School, which was partially covered by the avalanche, in some places to a depth of forty feet. The children while at their desks or playing were buried under the black slag. Other people were killed when the avalanche destroyed houses in Moy Street burying their unfortunate occupants alive.

Wales is a land inured to tragedy as so many of its families have been struck by loss of loved ones in a long succession of mining disasters. But the Aberfan tragedy had an agony peculiar to itself in its terrible toll of one hundred and twenty eight little children swept from life by the sable liquid avalanche of slag that poured down the mountain on to their school. The horror and poignancy of the subsequent scenes, when anguished parents and helpers tore at the massive mound trying to reach their buried children, was transmitted to all parts of the British Isles and abroad by the cameras of television teams. No one who saw these scenes will ever forget them.

Dr. J.C. Barker visited Aberfan on the day after the disaster. He was appalled by the devastation and suffering that he saw everywhere. While he helped, it occurred to him that there might have been people who had had premonitions of the disaster. Having been a keen student of psychical phenomena for many years it struck him that the unusual and especially tragic features of the Aberfan tragedy might provide an excellent opportunity to investigate precognition.

At Barker's request the science correspondent of the *London Evening Standard*, Peter Fairley, made an appeal in that newspaper on October 28, 1966, asking anyone who felt they had had any foreknowledge of the Aberfan disaster to communicate with him, describing their experiences. Many other newspapers, including psychic ones, syndicated the appeal. In addition the Psychophysical Research Unit at Oxford ran a press release asking for any cases of precognition of the disaster to be sent to them. In all, about 200 people claimed to have had some foreknowledge of the Aberfan disaster.

Dr. Barker himself received seventy six letters and began the long, tedious but necessary, process of replying not only to the writers but also to those witnesses who could offer confirmation, if possible, that the writer's experience had been told to them before the Aberfan disaster occurred. In due course, Dr. Barker received confirmation in twenty-four cases. His report appeared in the *Journal of the Society for Psychical Research in December* 1967. A more comprehensive report is lodged within the archives of the Society.

Space forbids reproduction of the majority of the cases but I will present three of them in addition to a table summarising some others.

*Case 1*

Eryl Mai Jones, aged ten, was a pupil at Pantglas School. She was the youngest daughter of Trevor and Megan Jones. Unfortunately she died on that fateful day. A local minister, the Rev. Glannant Jones, compiled a report of the case. Both parents read it and signed it as correct in the minister's presence.

She was an attractive dependable child, not given to imagination. A fortnight before the disaster she said to her mother, 'Mummy, I'm not afraid to die'. Her mother replied, 'Why do you talk of dying, and you so young; do you want a lollipop?'

'No', she said, 'But I shall be with Peter and June'. (Schoolmates.) The day before the disaster she said to her mother, 'Mummy, let me tell you about my dream last night'. Her mother answered gently, 'Darling, I've no time now, tell me again later'. The child replied, 'No, Mummy, you must listen. I dreamt I went to school and there was no school there. Something black had come down all over it!'

The next day she went off to school as usual in her normal happy manner. After the tragedy it transpired that she was subsequently buried in a communal grave with Peter on one side and June on the other. This last point may not, however, be significant, since the order of burial was apparently influenced by parents' requests.

*Case 2*

This case seemed to involve clairvoyance and/or clairaudience. Mrs. Constance Milder, aged forty seven, of Trevone Gardens, Manodan Vale, Plymouth wrote,

'I actually "saw" this disaster the night before it happened and the next day I had already told my next door neighbour about it before the news was broadcast.

'First, I "saw" an old school house nestling in a valley, then a Welsh miner, then an avalanche of coal hurtling down a mountain-side. At the bottom of this mountain of hurtling coal was a little boy with a long fringe looking absolutely terrified to death. Then for a while I "saw" rescue operations taking place. I had an impression that the little boy was left behind and saved. He looked so grief-stricken I could never forget him, and also with him was one of the rescue workers wearing an unusual peaked cap'.

Mrs. C.M. described her vision at a "Private Circle Meeting" held in a church on 20th October, 1966. This was confirmed in writing by six witnesses, and Mrs. C.M.'s neighbour Mrs.V.M. testified that Mrs. C.M. informed her of her vision at 8:30 a.m. on the 21st October, forty-five minutes before the actual disaster.

Mrs. C.M. continued: 'Now this is probably stranger still. Whilst looking at "The Mountain that Moved" on television on Sunday evening I saw both the terrified little boy talking to a reporter and also the rescuer I had seen in my vision. Of course it was not until I heard the tragic news that the full force of what I had seen came to me. It took me quite a while to get over the shock. This is not the first time I have foreseen events before they have occurred. Although the Aberfan disaster was the most outstanding'.

*Case 3*

Mrs. Mary Hennessy, aged 54, of 6 Chester Terrace, Barbican Road, Barnstaple, North Devon wrote:

The night before the Aberfan disaster I dreamt of a lot of children in two rooms. After a while some of the children joined some others in an oblong-shaped room and were in different little groups. At the end of the room there were long pieces of wood or wooden bars. The children were trying somehow to get over the top or through the bars. I tried to warn someone by calling out, but before I could do so one little child just slipped out of sight. I myself was not in either of the rooms, but was watching from the corridor. The next thing in my dream was hundreds of people all running to the same place. The look on peoples' faces was terrible. Some were crying and others holding handkerchiefs to their faces. It frightened me so much that it woke me up.

'I wanted to get out of bed and telephone my son and his wife and ask them to take special care of my two little granddaughters. When I did get up it was 6.45 a.m. I told my brother-in-law that I had had this terrible dream and that I was going to telephone my son and daughter-in-law but he said it was too early. I therefore waited until 8.45 a.m. and telephoned, telling them about my dream and that I was very worried as the dream was about children. I told them it wasn't our two little girls in the dream, as they looked more like schoolchildren.

The dream upset me very much all the next day. I did not hear about the Aberfan disaster until 5:I5 p.m.

Mrs. M.H'.s dream was verified in detail by her daughter-in-law Mrs. P.H. who confirmed that Mrs. M.H. had telephoned her before 9:00 a.m. on the day of the Aberfan disaster requesting her to take special care of her two small daughters.

In a careful analysis of the set of cases, Dr. Barker drew attention to a number of features that seemed noteworthy to him. Thirty-six of the letters were from dreamers. Others said they had had visions of the disaster or parts of it; some felt various degrees of unease for a period of time before the event. In some instances the dreams were so vivid and the feelings of horror and fear invoked in the dreamer so intense that the dreamer woke screaming. In a number of cases the dream was so impressive it haunted the dreamer for days. A number reported the screaming of children as a feature of their dream.

In seven cases, from four men and three women, Barker noted that 'they developed non-specific symptoms of acute mental and physical unease from four days to a few hours before the Aberfan disaster. Symptoms were in general characteristic of an acute anxiety state, and in five instances were either witnessed or reported to others before the disaster occurred, or before the percipients became aware of it.

Three percipients developed a sense of oppression and two experienced dyspnoea, choking sensations and feelings of suffocation before the disaster. Their distress was in all instances apparently relieved by the occurrence of the disaster or upon hearing news of it'.

Many of his correspondents told him that they had had previous premonitions in their lives about other disasters and some claimed that the attendant feelings Barker called the Pre-disaster Syndrome accompanied them. It was in fact a stamp of authenticity for the premonition.

In this respect a case brought to my notice is of interest and is by no means unique. A young lady, whose father worked with building contractors, became convinced one morning by her feelings of acute anxiety that her father would be in extreme danger later that day. There was no reason for her to entertain this fear but as the morning passed her distress increased to such an extent that she was driven to phone his company to warn him to take care.

Unfortunately the father's work was such that he himself planned which building sites he would visit at any given time and head office was unable to help her very much. She kept trying to ring various phone numbers, her acute forebodings by now causing her to drop any work of her own. She continued until four o'clock without success when suddenly the feelings left her, she calmed down and only then realised how irrational her efforts had been. Later that day the family was notified that at four o'clock her father had been in a car accident in which he had suffered serious injuries.

J. Gaither Pratt has conjectured that 'individuals who have convincingly precognitised one or more future events are at least as common as left-handed people'. Barker called such people 'human seismographs,' reacting by dream, vision and associated pre-disaster syndrome to a future catastrophe. He argued that if such people existed it might be possible to set up a Disaster Early Warning System and quoted Louisa Rhine who wrote in 1961, 'If the precognitive ability is developed and directed and if imperfect ESP impressions, especially those suggesting disaster ahead could be clarified, intelligent preventative action could follow to the untold advantage of mankind'.

This idea that a central bureau should collect and collate ostensible forewarnings of disasters raises a number of important questions, the most basic of which is that of querying the authenticity of such alleged premonitions. Confining ourselves to the Aberfan disaster we may ask how convinced we are by the evidence that one or more people received is 'glimpses' of the future tragedy. The word 'glimpses' is perhaps very appropriate when we appreciate that not one person got a complete picture of the event.

Several dreams undoubtedly resembled the disaster or part of it, a number of dreamers claiming to have subsequently recognised some of the harrowing TV and press pictures shown later. Most of the dreams were straightforwardly narrative; only a few were symbolic. The usual dream mechanisms – substitution of members of the dreamer's family or her home for the actual victims or place – seemed to occur. In summary, the following elements are among those that occurred in the ostensible premonitions: children screaming; wearing Welsh national costume; dying; Wales; a Welsh miner; mountains; valleys; Aberfan and desolate rows of houses; a black mountain slipping; horror; buried houses; a school; hundreds of black horses thundering down a hillside dragging hearses; avalanche of coal burying screaming children, etc.

Such a summary does not produce the impression of a strong correlation gained on reading the individual accounts. A simple test is instructive. If such detailed dreams and visions, accompanied by the feelings of horror, depression and misery, had occurred after the Aberfan tragedy, most people would probably conclude without hesitation that they were effect and the tragedy was the cause. But because of the fact that they were reported as having occurred prior to the disaster, we hesitate – rightly – at ascribing them to premonitions of Aberfan.

Certainly, they provide all the elements of the disaster. If, moreover, a Premonition Bureau had received them within a period of a week or two before the event, there seems little doubt, especially if the Bureau had already recognised the psychic reliability of some of its correspondents, that some action could have been taken to prevent the coming disaster or at least prevent the appalling loss of young children's lives at Aberfan.

And there, of course, we encounter again the intriguing Chinese puzzle-box question of whether or not a premonition's warning can be acted upon to avoid or prevent a disaster. Can one prevent a disaster from a premonition?

This leaves us in a Catch 22 situation. Ideally, what would constitute the perfect premonition, as far as the parapsychologist and a Premonitions Bureau are concerned? We can do no better than start with G.W. Lambert's five criteria, laid down in 1965 that he considered necessary to establish an undoubted connection between a dream and a future event.

1. The dream should be reported to a credible witness before the occurrence of the event to which it appears to relate.
2. The time interval between the dream and the event should be short.
3. The event should be one in which the circumstances of the dreamer seemed improbable at the time of the dream.
4. The description in the dream should be of an event destined to be fulfilled literally and not merely symbolically foreshadowed.
5. The details of the dream should tally with the details of the event.

The following comments seem relevant.

We have to remember that not all ostensible premonitions occur in dreams although sleep does appear to be the state in which most occur. People have claimed to have had these precognitive experiences in that peculiar state of consciousness just before falling asleep or just before a full awakening from sleep. The former often provides the subject with so-called hypnogogic phenomena; the latter provides similar phenomena termed hypnopompic. In addition, ostensible precognitions have been reported as being experienced in a fully awake, but relaxed, detached state when the subject is day-dreaming or reading or watching TV, etc. when the mind is calm. The restriction of the criteria to 'dreams' is therefore unnecessary and with that thinking we might lose a number of good cases.

Certainly any experience should be reported to more than one witness if possible: it should also be written down as soon as possible and a copy posted to the Society for Psychical Research in London. Dr. Donald J. West, a former research officer of the SPR remarked: 'If the impression is strong enough for the percipient to tell other people about it at once (as is often the case, according to the published accounts), there is no reason why he should not also tell the Society. He is in fact assuming that percipients have ever heard of the SPR.

The second criterion's stipulation is that the time interval between the dream and the event should be short is sensible. The longer the time interval, other things being equal, the more probable it is that coincidence would be the likely explanation. Certainly most ostensible premonitions occur within a few weeks before the event, which they are alleged to be related to, although there are on record some striking ones where many years have elapsed between premonitions and fulfilling events. Perhaps the difference between premonitions and revelations, as earlier discussed.

The third criterion states that really unusual events predicted are of more value than everyday examples while the last two criteria are also sensibly tailored to lend weight to the authenticity of the premonition. Having said that, we must admit that it would be the greatest of good fortune from the psychical researcher's point of view to find a case that satisfies all five criteria.

Many of the Aberfan cases are seen to satisfy several of the five criteria as shown from the data. Fourteen of the dreams fulfil number 1, while two others were pre-recorded. Most of the dreams occurred within a week of the Aberfan disaster, thus definitely fulfilling the short time interval defined in criterion number 2. And certainly criterion 3 is satisfied by the majority of cases and in many cases, the remaining two criteria were also satisfied.

All in all, the investigation carried out by Dr. Barker would seem to stand as a body of convincing evidence that for some human beings there is such a thing as a sort of 'timequake' that sends out its reverberations against the accepted direction of time's arrow, providing them with the knowledge of the forthcoming event. Or has it to do, in some way, with the depths of the subsequent emotions that are about to erupt? Who knows?

If a tragedy such as Aberfan with a death-toll of 148 can somehow cause premonitions, great wars and revolutions with their mass slaughter of human beings should likewise arouse anticipatory distress. There is actually some evidence in support of this view. But for now here is an overview of some further premonitions regarding Aberfan. I think that this makes the pattern of evidence clearer.

| Case | Percipient | Age | Time before disaster | Brief of experience | Verification of event |
|---|---|---|---|---|---|
| 1 | Mrs. G.E., Sidcup | 54 | 1 week | Dream of screaming children buried by avalanche of coal in mining village. Woke up screaming. | Confirmed by a friend |
| 2 | Mrs. S.A., St. Albans | 19 | 2 weeks | Dream of school, screaming children and 'creeping black slimy substance'. | Confirmed by husband |
| 3 | Mr. J.T., Stacksteads, Lancs. | 63 | 1 ½ days | Dream of name Aberfan and desolate rows of houses. | Not confirmed |
| 4 | Miss S.B., London | 11 | 2 months | Dream of school on hillside, avalanche and dying children. | Not confirmed |
| 5 | Miss E.R., Sheffield | 57 | 12 hours | Vision of school disaster and children in Welsh National costume going to heaven. | Confirmed by husband |
| 6 | Mrs. B.C. Smith, Cardiff | | 1 week | 'Spirit message' about 100 children being engulfed in black mud. | Confirmed by 1 witness |
| 7 | Mrs. J.R. | 65 | 6 weeks | Dream of scenery resembling | Confirmed by 2 witnesses |
| 8 | Mrs. E.B., Ilford | 58 | 2 weeks | Dream of crowds of people on hillside. Mud everywhere. Man holding lamp with little boy beside him. | Confirmed by 2 friends |
| 9 | Miss A.C., Leatherhead | 26 | 1 day | Dream of descending mountain with flowing surface. Rescued small screaming child. | Confirmed by 1 witness |

| Case | Percipient | Age | Time before disaster | Brief of experience | Verification of event |
|---|---|---|---|---|---|
| 10 | Mrs. L.S., Thetford. | 48 | 5 weeks | Dream of trees and logs hurling down hillside onto houses. Screams for help. | Pre-recorded in letter dated 18th Sept., 1966 |
| 11 | Mrs. E.S., London | 36 | 4 days | Dream of little boy buried up to neck in ground. Rescued. | Pre-recorded note-book |
| 12 | Mrs. L.H., Ealing | 68 | 2 weeks | Frightening dream of children standing below black mountain. Hundreds of black horses then thunder down hillside dragging hearses. | Confirmed by 3 |
| 13 | Mrs. S.B., Brighton. | 25 | Few hours | Nightmare of screaming child in telephone box. Followed child to a house enshrouded in black steam. | Confirmed by 1 |
| 14 | Mrs. E. P., Cardiff | | 2 hours | Dream of mountain of moving black shale and children's' screams. | Not confirmed |
| 15 | Mrs. R. H., Rhondda | 21 | 2 hours | Dream of dead and dying children on hillside | Not confirmed |
| 16 | Mrs. E.C. Coventry | | 2 weeks | 'Spirit message' forecast of avoidable manmade disaster connected with water. Many 'little bodies lying around'. | Confirmed by 4 witnesses |
| 17 | Mr. E.H., Newcastle-on-Tyne | 48 | 6 hours | Vivid fantasy of name 'Aberfan'. | Not confirmed |

| Case | Percipient | Age | Time before disaster | Brief of experience | Verification of event |
|---|---|---|---|---|---|
| 18 | Mrs. V.C. Ryde, I.O.W. | 63 | 3 weeks | Technicolor vision of little Welsh girl saying 'Aberredvan' | Not confirmed |
| 19 | Mrs. A.H., Normanton | | 10 months | 'Spirit message' about colliery disaster, moving mountain and children. | Confirmed by 1 witness |
| 20 | Mrs. J.A., Luton | 43 | 3 days | Dream of cross-shaped communal grave at bottom of hill. | Confirmed by husband and daughter |
| 21 | Mrs. E.G., London | 39 | 1 day | Dream of falling debris and crowds of men digging. | Confirmed by sister |
| 22 | Mrs. C.F., Aylesbury | 52 | 2 days | Nightmare of being smothered in 'deep blackness'. | Confirmed by a friend |
| 23 | Mrs. E.S., Parkstone | 73 | 2 days | Unpleasant dream of people running, crying and holding their heads. House 'tipping up'. | Confirmed by a friend |
| 24 | Mrs. S.H., Rayleigh | 64 | 1 day | Vivid dream of blackness, hearing voices and pressure of people claimed Similar experiences before other disasters. | Confirmed by a friend |

These are but a small sample, but I believe that in the case of Aberfan disaster there are enough of these reasonably ostensible precognitions to make us, at the very least, pause for thought.

You may remember I previously mentioned that emotion appears to be necessary within some areas of paranormality. This appears to be one of these situations, as though a wave of impending sadness sweeps before the actual event.

## *Don't Take the Train*

The cases so far described have dealt with ostensible precognitions where the invasion of the conscious mind has been dramatic and accompanied by visual and other sensory mode details. However, it appears that it is not always like this. At times it seems to be that the subconscious mind is the smarter big brother giving us a warning of a potential disaster to come.

W.G. Cox carried out an important study in which he paid particular attention to an examination of the hypothesis that precognition or premonitions may never reach the conscious mind in a recognisable form but may yet be strong enough to influence a person's actions. Cox selected a number of railway passenger trains involved in major accidents and obtained data regarding the total number of passengers who were on the specific trains. He ascertained in the last routine count made prior to the accidents that the total number on board the trains on the same run during each of the preceding seven days, and on the 14th, 21st and 28th days preceding was pretty constant, but on the day of the accidents there were considerably fewer passengers.

It so happens that in the United States of America the required data are available, being routinely kept on file for a number of years by many railroad companies.

Cox conducted his research for Coaches and Pullmans (i.e. sleepers) separately because (1) most Pullman figures are recorded by the Pullman Company of New York and (2) Pullman passengers normally book in advance while Coach passengers do not. So this provides mixed methods of booking. The same pattern held true for both: the passenger numbers were considerably less on the day of the individual accidents.

As an addendum, even in the case of the three hundred foot bridge that collapsed in Italy, near Genoa, in August 2018, the death toll could have been so much worse. This bridge spanned two railway lines underneath it, houses and a river; a very heavily trafficked situation all round and yet, when the bridge did collapse, there were no trains underneath it and no boats on the river. Maybe another case of latent pre-disaster syndrome – just a thought – who knows?

In all of the above cases of precognition I wonder if the methodology in gaining the subliminal information is similar to that of remote viewing where, more often than not, the 'perceiver' has little or no emotional ties to the situations. I certainly do not know the answer, but my thoughts are that this has little to do with the departed.

Nevertheless, it does appear that ordinary human beings can, on occasion, get a sense of future events albeit at a subliminal level.

As I indicated earlier, I do not really like the idea of premonitions as it makes me uneasy in my comfort zone, but that is just my own cognitive dissonance and I have to address the evidence in as scientific a manner as possible.

# 4

# EVP: Electronic Voice Phenomena

The general public first became widely aware of this means of communication also known as Instrumental Trans-Communication (ITC), largely due to Dr Konstantine Raudive, a Latvian writer and academic. In 1968 he published a very well received book in German about spirit voices that had ostensibly appeared on magnetic tape recorders. This book was translated into English in 1971 titled *Breakthrough.*

Raudive was well respected by his fellow philosophers and, interestingly, his four previously published books also addressed, in part, the idea and issues related to a potential life after death.

In *Breakthrough* he described one of the methods used to try to capture these voices on tape. They used a background of 'white noise' during the experimentation. It would appear that this type of sound acted as a sort of carrier wave that could be used in some way as a catalyst for the voices; maybe a type of audio surfing on this carrier-wave. White noise is similar to a sort of hiss, such as the sound that comes from a large waterfall. In these experiments the white noise was produced by tuning a radio to produce only radio static, which is a random mixture of sounds from different wavelengths.

The voices captured in this way were, in general, very faint and not really clear. He also noted that the voices seemed to speak at twice the speed of a normal human voice. As part of his experimentation, in order to eliminate the possibility that he was deluded or making a mistake, he then enlisted very credible people to take part on various panels of critical listeners. Among those enlisted were Professor Hans Bender, Dr Jule Eisenbud, (You will be hearing more about him later) Dr Karlis Osis and Professor Walter Uphoff along with a wide range of other professional people. A good researcher really can't do better than this.

Raudive's interest in this subject was first aroused when he read the results of experimentation in this field by Friedrich Jurgenson, a Swedish film director, who, when recording bird songs at night for a documentary, was often puzzled by the fact that random human voices appeared on the recordings. He then recognised that far from being random they appeared to be addressing him personally. He found that this method produced repeatable results, although not really experimentally 'controlled' in the truest sense. Jurgenson wrote two books on his findings, *Voices from the Universe* and *Radio Communications with the Dead.*

It is extremely interesting and, I think, important to note that within the experimentation of Raudive and Jurgensen the voices spoke in many languages.

As the phenomenon became better known it attracted many eager researchers including the following notable examples.

## *Marcello Bacci*

We now move on to a different methodology for contacting the departed when we look at the work of Marchello Bacci. He used an old style Normende valve radio to communicate. He called his work DRV – Direct Radio Voice. Once again a background of white noise proved to be needed before communication could take place.

In 1860 the Scottish physicist James Clerk Maxwell predicted the existence of radio waves. In 1902 Marconi was said to have sent the first successful radio telegraph message from England to Newfoundland – and so it began. No one could have predicted or dreamt that radio waves might eventually add to the wealth of evidence supporting an afterlife by way of contacting the consciousness of those who have passed: not only by listening to the voices of people who had died, but by introducing the possibility of having an interactive conversation with them, which would show comprehension and intelligent thought responses in that actual time frame.

As an aside, when Clerk Maxwell was at school he was always asking teachers seemingly stupid questions, which probed more and more into the subject at hand. A Scottish word for stupid is *daft.* At school he gained the nickname 'Daftie' Maxwell, but the last laugh was with him as he turned out to be a brilliant physicist. The moral of the story is never to be afraid to ask a seemingly daft question.

Bacci received discarnate voices through his radio and, in the early 1970s, the quality was similar to that of Raudive and Jurgenson, but by the late '70s they were very much clearer. He held demonstrations in his own home and had audiences of up to seventy people. Visitors were often directly addressed by their deceased loved ones. Many researchers from around the world attended sessions with Bacci and were so impressed that they asked permission to use the radio themselves. Permission was granted, but in every session where Bacci was absent there were no positive results. This may sound a bit fishy but we are told that Bacci himself was a very good medium. To this date no one has worked out why communication is possible with an ostensible afterlife using an old valve radio tuned into white noise in the short wave band. It seems especially strange as Bacci seemed to be some kind of necessary catalyst.

Now this is where your credibility may be stretched, under the category of unbelievable.

In 2004 a controlled experiment was carried out in Grossetto in the presence of thirty-seven people including scientists, investigators and technicians. Some of the audience were mothers who had lost children. Before and after the experiment the radio was thoroughly examined and it was confirmed that there was no external access to it through the bench that it was sitting on or anywhere else. The radio was in such a position that it was visible from all sides, and there was no back on it.

The public in attendance had to sit a metre and a half behind Bacci and the investigators.

My dear colleague Professor David Fontana sat at the left hand side of Bacci, who was directly in front of the radio. The respected Dr Anabela Cardoso was immediately behind David, looking over his left shoulder and a Mr Robin Foy was on Bacci's right hand side.

Analogue and digital audio recorders along with video recorders were set up to document the session. Bacci turned his radio on and slowly tuned it to a range of seven to nine Megahertz thus producing white noise. After about twenty minutes he stopped tuning and a sound was produced, described as a vortex-like sound like wind or waves. The first communications were in Italian. Bacci spoke to the radio telling 'them' that they could also speak in Spanish, Portuguese and English. The voices then addressed Fontana and Foy in English and Cardoso in Spanish.

Members of the audience then received messages in different languages, some of them with that distorted sound of ITC voices, some a bit clearer. This session lasted about an hour. Then a Professor Festa and a technician removed two of the valves from the radio but the voices continued!

Then they removed all five valves from the radio – in clear sight of everybody – and the voices still continued as before with the same volume and clarity. Without warning Bacci then turned the radio off and, to the amazement of all, the communication continued for another two minutes and twenty seconds. Bacci's radio was then turned at an angle of 90 degrees and closely inspected by all. Some sceptics, quite sensibly, proposed that the voices could have been transmitted to the radio from an external source, even in the absence of any visual receiver.

All recorded voices were subsequently tested and certified through endorsed FBI voice print analysis software, which was then deemed to confirm that the voices could not have been produced by fraudulent transmissions. The sceptics were still not satisfied.

With this in mind a Dr Emanuelo Toriello conducted further investigations with Bacci and placed the radio inside a special shield that blocked all radio signals. And yet the voices continued!

(I resist the temptation to smile.)

Marcello Bacci passed away on the July 15, 2019. He left a wonderful legacy and will be fondly remembered.

## *George Meek*

George W. Meek headed a foundation called Metascience, based in North Carolina. It was an organisation engaged in research into the paranormal. Meek was fortunate enough to have attracted over forty professional and technical people to Metascience. Included in its membership were physicists, nuclear chemists, biochemists and psychiatrists who were all keenly interested in examining all types of phenomena that defied explanation by conventional science.

Meek himself was a successful design engineer and business executive; his areas of expertise included designing air conditioning systems, water coolers, thermal pollution devices and waste water devices. Not a person, one would feel, with his head in the clouds nor a person prone to embark on flights of fancy. He was able to retire at sixty years of age when he turned his hand fully to investigating and researching the idea of life after death. He approached this quest both as an engineer and scientist.

When reporting on this type of work one has to remember that the stranger the claims are, the greater the need for caution and reliable documentation. John G Fuller, one of my favourite authors, took up the challenge of investigating the claims of George Meek. He did so from a very cautious standpoint. His investigations took him to Germany, Switzerland and Great Britain. On reflection Fuller said that he did not realize the complexity of the task that he had undertaken and wondered, had he known, if he would do it again. I, for one, am so glad that he did take up that challenge.

In one of Meek's experimental séance group sessions in Philadelphia, a deceased scientist identified himself through the medium. The purported entity claimed that he wanted to 'Co-operate with living engineers to develop an electromagnetic communication system between those living on the earth level and the discarnate state in which he now existed'.

This reminds me a little of Tesla who purported to come through a medium in the Scole group. He displayed an interest in speaking to a colleague of mine, Professor Arthur Ellison, who was an electrical engineer.

In the case of the Philadelphia group their first quest was to establish the authenticity of the purported communicator. The medium was a sober and serious advertising executive at one of the largest companies in the country. The discarnate person claimed to be a physics professor from Yale, namely one William Frances Gray Swann. The group investigated the information given to them from this communicator and, after checking a long series of facts that were given about his background, qualifications, life events etc., became more convinced that they were indeed receiving valid information. Swann then provided detailed information about how communication might be accomplished through an electronic channel *without* the use of a medium. Yes, they too had to have a medium present for the communication to work.

This steeled Meek's determination to make a breakthrough in this field.

It was estimated that the equipment needed to seriously continue this research work would cost in the region of $70,000. He was fortunate enough to raise this money from Jim McDonnell, chairman of the board of McDonnell Douglas.

## *The next step*

It was seven years into his research in this field when Meek encountered Bill O'Neil, an eighth grade dropout who was an electronics whiz kid. Not only that, he was the best clairaudient and clairvoyant that Meek had come across. No one else had made that impression. O'Neil had also previously carried out some experiments of his own.

In one of O'Neil's experiments a communicator came through and identified himself as a 'Doc Nick', a former ham radio operator who claimed to have died five years earlier. He gave instructions to O'Neill to demonstrate how certain audio frequencies could act as an energy source. When these frequencies were combined with a tape recorder, voice contact could be made with him. Again, O'Neil's presence seemed vital to the success of any session. Within these experimental sessions that were recorded on tape, O'Neil would ask a question and Doc Nick would answer.

Meek listened to one of these tapes and was mildly impressed, although the voice did sound somewhat robotic. O'Neil suggested the name Spiricom for this work. Meek was not too keen on that suggestion, but continued with the experiments. It was not helped by the fact that O'Neil was not the easiest person to get along with, in a sense like Croiset who was mentioned earlier in this book.

Not long after Meek began his research work with O'Neil, Doc Nick was soon replaced by another communicator, Dr George Mueller, who had been a competent engineer and physicist. He told the research team, through O'Neil, where they could locate his death certificate, issued in 1967.

He also provided them with his Social Security number and details of his activities at the University of Wisconsin. All of these pieces of information proved to be absolutely correct.

I find that very impressive and I have no reason to doubt the validity of this report.

He then gave them further instruction as to how they could refine their equipment and by 1980 the quality of communication was much clearer and less distorted.

I will give you a small sample of the type of conversation that was then recorded on tape. I don't expect all of you to understand it, but stick with it ... the personality exchange is interesting.

Mueller: I think the big problem is an impedance mismatch into that third transistor.
O'Neil: Third transistor?
Mueller: Yes. The transistor that follows the input.
O'Neil: I don't understand.
Mueller: (impatiently) The pre-amp, the pre-amp!
O'Neil: Oh, the pre-amp
Mueller: I am not sure, with a 150 ohm, one half watt resistor in parallel with a .0047 microfarad ceramic capacitor I think we can overcome the impedance mismatch.
O'Neil: Oh boy, I'll have to get the schematic back.
Mueller: You'd rather have the schematic?
O'Neil: I'd rather mark it on the schematic, Doctor.

Neither seemed too impressed with the other and so it continued.

Further technical information can be found in J. J. Fuller's book, *The Ghost of 29 Megacycles.*

As time passed it became clear that the system would not work without the use of a physical human medium. The communicator, Mueller, gradually faded away – the reason given was that he was heading further up a spiritual pathway.

To that extent, Meek's 'dream' of having to dispense with mediums to contact the departed through electronic means did not come to fruition and Spiricom fell silent.

However in 1982 it was announced that, 'Meek would release, without patent, full details of his equipment – including wiring diagrams'. His admirable goal was to encourage other researchers to replicate his efforts and expand on them.

George Meek did indeed subsequently provide all the relevant data.

## *Hans Otto König*

Upon the release of Meek's data, many people were encouraged to continue with his work. Everyone was anxious to take this whole exciting idea further, using Meek's methodology to achieve the dream of a medium free two-way dialogue with the departed.

One very successful person in this field was Hans Otto König, a private consultant to German industry in the electro-acoustical field who had already been studying this idea of background noise as a facilitator in these types of experiments. Upon reviewing a selection of previous experiments he noted that, no matter the method, all of them used frequencies that pushed into the ultrasonic range. Most magnetic tape recorders don't go beyond 20,000 Hertz. With that in mind he had, a few years earlier, designed equipment that reached 30,000 Hertz, using a complex mixture of frequencies and harmonics from four generators. This was beyond the audible hearing range for humans. He called his device König's Generator.

It was reported that his experiments then proved to be quite successful.

In 1983 he was invited to give a 'live on air' demonstration of his equipment on Radio Luxembourg. When he arrived at the studio he was carefully watched at all times by the station's engineers and the presenter, one Rainer Holbe. No one, including König, was sure of what would happen – no rehearsal – just an announcement that he would try to make a two way contact with 'someone' who had passed over, without the use of a medium'.

They were now live on air; one of the staff asked if a voice could come through in direct response to a request. Within a few seconds a voice came through and said, 'Otto König makes wireless with the dead'.

Another question was asked, another pause, and then a voice came through the speaker saying, 'We hear your voice'.

The programme presenter's voice was shaking when he said, 'Dear listeners, I swear by the life of my children that nothing has been manipulated. There are no tricks'.

The replies through the equipment were as clear as the questions asked. This was obviously a great step forward. Everyone present accepted that the voices were 'paranormal' in the sense that they were not produced by any normally understood or accepted means.

Subsequently Meek, along with other guests, met with König and sat in session with him. He noted that when the equipment was switched 'on' there was a faint background noise, but nothing like the noise that the poor communicators had to speak over in his earlier experiments. After a silence a voice known to Meek said, 'Hello George'.... he felt a chill down his back as he recognised the voice as that of Dr George Mueller. One by one, more identifiable communicators spoke, providing relevant messages to the other guests.

Meek was stunned! This appeared to be a repeatable experiment; the gold standard of psychical research; the dream.

He returned home with new optimism and impetus to continue his work. This renewed energy spurred him on to find more researchers in Europe and USA who were both electronically savvy and preferably also psychic. In 1994 he founded the Life Beyond Death Foundation. In his own mind he theorised that if Mueller had 'moved up' in the spirit world to a higher frequency then maybe, just maybe, he might be able to contact him again through his further experimentation.

### *Dr Anabela Cardoso.*

Dr Cardoso, a senior diplomat, is among the current researchers in this field. She began her experiments around 1997 as a result of the death of a friend's son. Portuguese is her native language but she is a linguist, fluent in six languages, and was at one time Portugal's Charge d'Affairs in Japan and India.

She began with EVP using a white noise background, as did Jurgenson, but then moved to the use of old valve radios looking for DRV (direct radio voice).

Professor David Fontana attended one of her experimental sessions in Lyon where several excellent communications were coming through in Portuguese. He broke into this session and asked, 'Can you speak to me in English?' Immediately a voice came through, and although not of good quality, appeared to say, 'Help me prove I'm alive'. David then asked the communicators to repeat two phrases namely 'Hello David' and 'How are you?' The first reply was not at all clear but was followed much more clearly by 'Hello David' and 'How are you?'

As David said, 'There was no question that the replies came through the experimental radio'.

An important aspect of this test was that there was no warning given to the experimenter that David was going to ask for these phrases to be repeated.

Due to her success with DRV she founded, at her own expense, an international journal published in Portuguese, Spanish and English. This ITC Journal provides a forum for discussion on the latest serious findings in this field.

I have been fortunate enough to be able to include an up-to-date quote from Dr Cardoso.

'Years ago, at the end of the 1980s, communicators from another dimension informed the Luxembourg team, Maggy and Jules

Harsh-Fischbach, that soon ITC would be everywhere. The high entity that the earth operators called the Technician avowed that if not during the twentieth century, it would become true in the twenty-first century.

My own communicators from Rio do Tempo station work relentlessly with my radios and inform me that "We [they] are working to be able to speak with everybody in your world interested in our world". Thus, we need to wait patiently and hope their goal will indeed be attained.

We should keep in mind that although the success of ITC work lies primarily with the communicators, the harmony between the operators on the earth and the entities in the next dimension of life is fundamental for that work to succeed. We can rightly say that the main goal of Instrumental Transcommunication is to help with the expansion of human understanding of consciousness, but to understand ITC ways humanity first needs to attain a level of expanded consciousness. Both goals, albeit difficult to achieve and seemingly antagonistic, are indeed complementary. As the communicators have said, "We need humanity to grow spiritually to be able to establish strong ITC ties with the earth'.

## *Marcus Lang*

On July 14, 2019 I had the following communication from an Australian medium named Marcus Lang. I have not had any experience with him myself but do know others who hold him in high esteem. He provided me the following information.

> I have always been interested in radio communication since childhood. My spirit team said they are influenced by the work of Marcelo Bacci, whom I also admire. Actually, our mediumship is quite similar. So the spirit team told us they would like to experiment with radio to create a bridge that can be used to facilitate two-way communications between the realms – Spirit to earth frequency.
>
> I was advised to purchase two Apple watches series 4. They have a walkie-talkie function that is easy to use by pressing the appropriate icon and the other watch will answer. This creates a radio wave between the two, if in range of the associated iPhones. Bluetooth is the radio carrier. If not then the cell network is utilised.
>
> Troy is the spirit technician in my spirit team, responsible for séance phenomena. He found a way that he was able to make

one watch signal the second when he wanted us to initiate the walkie-talkie function. My wife would do that and I would answer and listen on my end. Being the medium I need to be on the receiving end. After a few tries with nothing happening, I heard a voice speaking out of the speaker in my watch. This was Troy. The first few times were brief but gradually increased in time and clarity of speech. Unfortunately this was difficult because we had to actively hold open the talkie function to keep the carrier wave (radio wave) active. Troy would imprint his speech into that open carrier wave.

After some weeks of this he worked out how to make a telephone call from watch A, to my watch, B. I would answer and listen and he would say hello and I replied. This we found was a much easier and cleaner radio wave to use for his voice imprint. We were then able to have short conversations.

He would then cause my watch walkie-talkie feature to come on as a signal for us to initiate a cell call, or he would do that after the signal so we could find a quiet spot and have the two watches far enough apart that feedback wasn't an issue. This occurred at unexpected times: once at the dinner table with my mother and sister present where they were able to listen in on my phone call from Troy. They were amazed. This would also happen just as we are getting into the car to go out, and even while I was in the bathroom. It has to happen when they (spirit side) have the energy in tune with the frequency of the cell call radio wave. It is a case of when they are ready, not so much when we are.

After practising this over some weeks, we can now sustain a call for as long as five minutes. The voice is usually accompanied by a whooshing sound as he continually adjusts the frequency of his vibration, much like Bacci did with his valve radios, but this time it's being done on spirit side. The words are usually slowly spoken, often whispery, and at times difficult to understand. Sometimes it is very clear and we talk about their plans to use microwave radio waves in the future. They even told me the specific radio receiver needed for this, down to identifying the model number. I will get that sometime this year, as it is very expensive. In the meantime this is very good practice for all of us. If conditions are good, the speech is excellent, albeit, sounding typically as voices often do in a physical séance. If conditions aren't so good, it is difficult to understand but always it is practice.

I was given permission to start recording our conversations and I have been able to record the first one, which I shared publicly among peers and friends interested. What is heard often and well are the remarks from the team to me as how much they love me and need me as their medium. This was also shared publicly.

As I now purchase more professional equipment, such as a studio microphone, I can record directly to the computer, and soon with a video camera I can document each phone call and will be able to record with far better clarity. If the correct conditions required can be achieved on this side also, on a mediumistic and vibrational level, the calls will improve and I can show this improvement as I share our progress publicly. People will be able to hear that direct, two-way conversations are occurring between our spirit technician, Troy and myself.

I believe it won't be long before we can use this open channel of communication. Imagine a bridge that goes through the veil from our side to theirs. The intent is to be able to bring in loved ones on the other side of life, to be met by their family on this side of life, to be able to speak to their beloved children, husbands etc., who have left the earth, in their own recognisable voices they had while on earth. This should bring healing to broken hearts. Technology is the way forward in spirit communication in this 21st century. As everyone has access to this technology in their purses and pockets, perhaps someday these devices will be the medium that will be needed.

Proof of concept is done. We have witnesses to the calls. I really need to thank Marcello Bacci for leading the way in this work. We hope to emulate his work in a more modern way.

We hope so too, Marcus. It would exciting to think that the most up to date watches might in fact be a suitable means of communication with the departed in the future, even although it does sound a bit Sci-fi at the present time.

In 2018 Dr Sean Richards reviewed past research in this field and discovered, as a sort of spin-off, that hundreds of spontaneous EVP messages had been left on a flight simulation programme on his computer. This is similar to the phenomena reported by Locher and Fischbach in Luxemburg in the 1990s.

Over the years, other researchers have also tried to develop a *psychophone,* a sort of broadband radio receiver that could simultaneously receive spirit voices in various languages. One such person was the incredible France Grierson, a man with unbelievable diverse psychic talents, who you will hear more about later in this book.

So there you have some background into this aspect of psychical research. Your head may well be hurting by now, but that is the way that things have progressed. In this book you will read about more challenges that researchers have encountered in their particular line of interest and the dedication that they have had just to keep going without fear or favour. Nobody said that this was easy!

The problem with psychical research is not that there is no evidence for any particular claim in any avenue of the paranormal, but that there is such a diverse spectrum of phenomena to examine within each topic. This holds true, whether the individual phenomenon pertains to add to a survival hypothesis or to the amazing talents that we may hold as ordinary human beings. This is often why antagonistic critics expound generalities without having actually examined a particular line of inquiry in depth, or indeed at all. The other tactic is to find a weak case and hold it up as a typical example of any particular phenomenon, thus dismissing it all as nonsense. This is why I always try to illustrate the best evidential cases.

Of course there are poor examples of anything in life: a bad car mechanic, a poor dentist, a poor teacher, etc., but that does not mean that there are not excellent examples in all of these areas. It is just the same with reports of paranormal phenomena.

That is why we have to choose reliable sources of information at all times.

I will now climb down from my high horse and continue with the next topic.

# 5

# Thoughtography

Thought projection onto film

It is all too easy for uninformed critics to wave aside reports of strange phenomena and abilities simply because they cannot conceive of them being true, especially since reliable documented evidence is available. Within the last few years I actually heard someone say from a public platform that my next 'gentleman' was found to be fraudulent. Really? I leave it to you to make up your own mind.

## *Ted Serios*

There are many difficult subjects to work with within the realms of psychical research, but I think that Ted Serios must win first prize.

It was brought to the attention of Dr Jule Eisenbud M.D., a well-respected psychiatrist and psychoanalyst, that a person called Ted Serios was claiming that he could project images onto Polaroid film simply by using the power of his mind. Eisenbud was intrigued. Suspecting a hoax he took on the extremely difficult, even tortuous, task of researching into this claim and subsequently conducted experiments with Serios over a three-year period.

I have to confess that when I read Eisenbud's accounts relating to his dealings with Serios my heart warmed to him. I felt such an affinity with him, both in his style of writing and his trials and tribulations in working with this very unusual man.

Serios was a poorly educated, unemployed Chicago bellhop in his early forties when Eisenbud first took an interest in him. This interest followed an article that he had read in Fate Magazine, by the Vice President of the Illinois Society for Psychical Research. The article described experiments that this Society had completed with Serios where images of the Taj Mahal, the Pentagon and the dome of the Whitehouse had been ostensibly thought-projected on to Polaroid film. It was even more intriguing as it was reported that in the final stages of the experimentation they had evolved and implemented a strict protocol whereby these experiments were eventually completed under conditions which would rule out any potential fraud: e.g. Serios was never allowed to touch the film that was itself supplied by a third party.

Eisenbud was also very interested in the fact that The Illinois Psychical Research Society had turned to a Mr Calderwood, the Vice President of the Polaroid Corporation, for advice and comment. Calderwood is quoted thus: 'Let me stress that while a clever man could tamper in advance with our film, I know of no way he could do it if you were to show up with the film you bought in a store; tampering with the film would be a long and complicated procedure and nothing could be done by sleight of hand without an opportunity to substitute something in front of or behind the lens'.

As Eisenbud was already an experienced researcher in paranormal matters, this report whetted his appetite; he was already very intrigued, interested and initially excited as here, at last, there might actually be a possibility and opportunity of carrying out a 'repeatable experiment'.

As already mentioned – the psychical researcher's dream.

Eisenbud thought it strange that he had never heard of Serios before and, after reading the aforesaid article, took it upon himself to contact Curtis Fuller, the President of the Illinois Society for Psychical Research. He subsequently received an invitation from Fuller to come to a demonstration with Serios in Chicago with the 'warning' that there was 'no guarantee, of course, that results would be forthcoming'.

This induced all sorts of negative thoughts in Eisenbud's mind, such as why did Polaroid not seem terribly interested in this phenomenon; what rigour did Fuller bring to the experimentation; why was the article in a magazine and not a recognised journal of parapsychology? With these questions in mind he responded to Fuller with a conventional 'brush-off' letter, 'Thank you, if I am ever in Chicago I shall let you know' and consigned Fuller's letter to the wastebasket.

About a month later Eisenbud was due to go on a lecture tour during which he could feasibly make a visit to Chicago to see Serios. This prompted him to contact Fuller to that end and he was pleased to be told that Serios would indeed see him, and to bring a Geiger counter. His contact was to be a Mrs Morris. Just before Eisenbud was to set out on his lecture tour he received the following letter from Fuller, 'I would like to add to your knowledge of Mr Serios' personal characteristics: he has a drinking problem. If we assume a priori that anyone who has a drinking problem may fail to keep appointments occasionally then you are taking a chance with him. However if you would like to have a more convincing demonstration you might like to bring along some pictures in sealed opaque envelopes and Ted could try to get pictures of these images. Ted prefers buildings'.

Eisenbud was none too happy at this point as one hour before his tour departure he realised that his ostensible 'star performer' might not even show up!

Things became even worse as unfortunately his lecture tour did not go as well as he expected and as he boarded the plane to meet Serios he, 'Couldn't have cared less about the alcoholic content of Ted's brain'. Somewhat jaded he eventually arrived at his hotel room in Chicago.

It had been agreed that Serios and Mrs Morris, along with an independent observer (Jon) would meet in his hotel room at 8pm that evening. Serios did turn up on time, and seemed somewhat disappointed that Eisenbud had not brought a Geiger counter. At this point no one knew why he wanted this item. Before proceedings got underway Eisenbud, possibly unwisely, asked everyone if they would like to order a drink. Ted looked nonchalantly and replied, 'If anyone else is going to have one I'll have a scotch on the rocks – make that a double if you don't mind!'

The first experimental session began.

Jon acted as a note-taker as well as an observer.

Eisenbud drew a fresh film pack from a sealed container in his bag and loaded it into a Polaroid Land 100 camera that he had brought with him. Drawing from his years of previous experience in investigating alleged sensitives/mediums, neither had been out of his possession for even a moment. This was considered to be a preliminary session, as Eisenbud did not really know what to expect.

8:50 p.m. Ted was 'ready to go' He smoked throughout the test session – result – blank film.

9:32 p.m. He was ready for his second try. From his pocket Ted pulled out, what he referred to as, his gismo. This was, for all the world, like the cardboard centre of a toilet roll with a piece of clear plastic over each end. This was carefully examined and held no surprises, although this all seemed unnecessarily complicated to Eisenbud.

Before every trial Serios would go into an intense state of concentration, with his eyes wide open and lips compressed. His body would shake and the foot of his crossed leg would twitch quite violently. His face would go blotchy and the veins would stand out on his forehead.

He would sometimes hold one end of the gismo to his head with the other end pointing at the virgin film; this supposedly helped his concentration.

Result of test 2: blank. At this point another double scotch was ordered 'for his cold'.

9:50 p.m. Test 3: blank.

10:24 p.m. Serios was ready for Test 4 again blank. They came to call the blanks a 'blackie'.

10:35 p.m. Test 5, another blackie.

It was at this point that things became a bit weirder ... as if they were not weird enough. Ted asked if he could take a shower in Eisenbud's hotel room.

This was agreeable and Ted left the room to have a shower. The people in the main room heard the shower going on and then off within a few minutes. It was at this point that Eisenbud was trying to work out if this was some sort of trickery but concluded that was not likely. Ted then put his head around the door and said, 'Hey Doc do you mind coming over here for a minute?' When Eisenbud approached the door Ted, in the nude, threw it wide open and asked, 'Hey Doc, do you mind if I use one of your bath towels? Eisenbud's experience as a psychoanalyst drew him to the conclusion that this was in line with a type of infantile narcissism often seen in psychics. His words, not mine!

11:04 p.m. Test 6: Ted claimed that his heart was pounding and that was a good sign. This film showed some amorphous fogging and a few lines or shadows.

11:05 p.m. Test 7: A blackie.

11:06 p.m. Test 8: Ted was very noticeably shaking. When Eisenbud grasped the film tab to pull it out for development he was overjoyed to see that there was a picture of a recognisable structure on the film. Mrs Morris recognised it as the Chicago Water Tower. Ted meantime was relaxed in his chair and staring into space as if nothing of this concerned him.

They continued taking another three shots up to 11:50 p.m. Each shot had 'something' on them but the last shot was very interesting as it had the word STEVENS visible on it as an illuminated neon sign. It turned out that this was similar to an old sign from the building that was now the Hilton hotel. It had not been known as Stevens for over thirty years and Ted had no particular memories attached to it. Eisenbud then chose to stop the session, as Ted's pulse was now one hundred and thirty two.

After this experimental session Eisenbud was most encouraged as he planned the next steps in his investigation.

It was obvious that Serios could indeed 'think' something onto Polaroid film.

Eisenbud's head was buzzing and he was again full of questions, such as, 'Why has no experimental unit ever seriously tested him? Why has no Psychical Researcher, Psychologist, et al., ever shown a real interest in him?' Especially curious as Ted himself was actually keen that 'scientists' should test him.

His next quest was to try to get answers to these, and other, questions.

Eisenbud was able to contact a Dr M., a psychologist, who had witnessed Ted's work for himself. He had been present when Ted had achieved some very positive results on film and was thus extremely impressed; he later made a statement to that effect. He, too, was frustrated that no responsible organisation had come forward to test Ted. He wrote, almost pleadingly, 'There is a crying need for this to happen!'

Dr M. in fact had been hired by a Dr R., the chief physicist of a research laboratory, to give a psychological evaluation of Serios. However when Eisenbud had an interview with Dr R. he felt that he was being fobbed off with 'political' type answers in a careful, too careful, weighing of words in a 5$^{th}$ amendment type of stance. Eisenbud sadly concluded that there was nothing achievable here.

Moving on, Eisenbud contacted a large weekly publication, which was at one time interested in Ted's abilities. He interviewed Mr Birch from the magazine as he, too, had previously witnessed excellent results from experimental sessions but he stated that the story was dead at the moment. When Eisenbud questioned him about an explanation as to why the interest in Ted had waned he replied, 'So the guy takes pictures with his mind, so what?'

I can imagine Eisenbud's thoughts!

His next attempt to consolidate his ideas about Ted's abilities was a real shocker. He contacted a Professor X, from the psychology department of a well-known Chicago university, who seemingly had several sessions with Ted the year before. Even although the results were rumoured to have been fairly successful, nothing more had been heard about them. On the day of his meeting with Professor X, he did admit that he had had several sessions with Ted and that he had indeed projected pictures on film by thought, and what did Eisenbud want to know?

Eisenbud asked, 'Were there any recognisable structures on the films?'

Answer, somewhat reluctantly, 'Well, yes'.

Eisenbud, 'Well why is it that your department has not taken this work further?'

Answer, 'In one crucial test he had been given a hidden target of a Miami hospital. He missed the target and a completely different building showed up on the film'.

Eisenbud, with a hint of sarcasm, 'You mean he got the *wrong* building?

Reply, 'Exactly'.

Eisenbud was flabbergasted by the insanity of that remark (After all Serios had 'thought' an image of a building onto film!!) and asked why they were not continuing their research. The reply was that research would take at least one afternoon a week, for possibly months.

Eisenbud said, 'so?'

Reply, 'Well it is not my research strategy or that of my department – not our dish of tea, that is'.

Eisenbud had to bite his tongue in frustration and anger as there was so much that he wished point out and comment on. The fact that Ted had reproduced a BUILDING on film at all by concentration was to say the least not 'normal'. There was no existing scientific model for such an event. Any good scientist should be interested in this and it should warrant further research, but Professor X seemed aloofly indifferent.

If I had been Eisenbud I would have been raging and no doubt a few swear words would be running through my head.

Regrouping, Eisenbud subsequently contacted a Mrs Ochler who had achieved very good results with Ted's thoughtography in the past.

When he met her she had brought a selection of pictures from her own research along with others that she had acquired from reliable sources. The images ranged from well-known structures such as the

Eiffel Tower, the Taj Mahal and the Pentagon. Ted had even achieved interior shots of the Whitehouse including one of JFK in his study. After lengthy discussions with Mrs Ochler, Eisenbud was hooked and decided to further investigate Serios himself. He then arranged for Ted to come to Denver a week later to participate in serious experimentation. This was to begin by having Ted undergo a thorough medical check up in his home town. In actual fact this did take place and his results were extremely normal – possibly surprising considering his lifestyle. The big day arrived for Ted to undertake serious research in Denver, but when Eisenbud saw Ted coming off the plane at Denver Airport his heart sank as it was obvious that he was legless and totally stoned.

Undaunted, he worked with Ted solidly for three years, setting up experiments etc. and greatly reduced his own bank balance in a quest for truth.

This wild stallion that was Ted Serios could not really be trained to perform to order, but he did achieve results from blurry images to much clearer pictures, as and when. So not in the truest sense a 'repeatable experiment' to order, but repeatable none the less.

But, regardless of anything, more than four hundred of Serios's psychic photographs contained specific images; as I said, sometimes a bit blurry but nonetheless recognisable. James, 'The amazing Randi', did try to 'duplicate' this work for television in conditions that barely resembled those of Eisenbud's experimentation. Serios, on occasion, would have to wear clothes supplied by the experimenters and was separated from the camera, which was sometimes in another room. Along with this he was sometimes enclosed in an electrically shielded Faraday cage. Randi's show on television and his dismissal of the Serios case was all it took for many people to happily think that it was fake. However as the highly respected Professor Stephen Braude states, 'If Randi had actually been able to do what Serios did, you can be sure he would have done it publically and with considerable fanfare ... but there is no documentary evidence of Randi even having attempted to duplicate the Serios phenomenon under anything like the conditions in which Serios succeeded'.

Braude also states that it also does not stop 'the well respected but despicably non-authoritative Martin Gardner' from claiming that Randi 'regularly' duplicates the Serios phenomenon, and with more skill'. This reminds me of the saying 'Never let the truth spoil a good story'.

In contrast, the three years of genuine rigidly controlled experiments with Eisenbud at the helm were witnessed by over twenty-five highly respected doctors and scientists, who found the phenomenon inexplicable in terms of conventional scientific paradigms. No conventional ideas or explanations could be proffered.

As far as I am aware, the avid sceptics, and some not quite so sceptical, have chosen to ignore the results achieved through Eisenbud's endeavours. Frustrating as that is, there is really no surprise there.

I call this the ostrich syndrome. I can't see it therefore it cannot be true.

As I said before, nobody said this was easy.

It is up to you, now, to make up your mind about all of this or perhaps investigate further for yourself.

I will finish this chapter with Eisenbud's description of Ted.

He called him, 'A weird little man who could have stepped right out of 'Grimm's Fairytales'.

If there were a medal for patience and tenacity within psychical research I would posthumously nominate Jule Eisenbud as a recipient.

Eisebud passed away in 1999.

PS: I never really found out why Ted wanted a Geiger counter at his sessions.

# 6

# Where There Is A Will

The Chaffin v Chaffin will case is probably one of the most widely quoted cases in the realms of psychical research. Subsequent to the discovery of a second will, it was the subject of great dispute, despite the fact that a court ruled that the second will was authentic. What has this to do with the paranormal I hear you ask? Well – the second will came to light after a materialised spirit was purported to have given a member of the family the location of the said will.

## *The Chaffin Family*

The Chaffin family, who farmed sugar cane and cotton, lived and still live, in and around Mocksville, a small country town in Davie County, North Carolina, some 400 miles south of New York. At this time the family consisted of James L Chaffin, his wife Rachel and their four sons in order of birth: John, James Pinkney, Marshall and Abner.

In November 1905, James Chaffin, then in his fifties, instructed his attorney to draw up a final will and testament in which he bequeathed his entire estate of one hundred and two acres to Marshall, his third son, with NO bequests to his wife or his other three sons. This will, dated November 16, was signed by him in the presence of two witnesses. The terms of this will were unknown to any of his sons except, just possibly, Marshall and his wife Susie.

Some sixteen years later on September 7, 1921 James Chaffin, aged about seventy, died as a result of a fall. As no other will could be found, the 1905 will was probated on September 24, 1921 and Marshall, who like his brothers had his own farm, duly inherited his father's estate in full. Whatever they felt about the will and its apparent unfairness, his brothers had no legal grounds on which to contest their lack of inheritance.

The terms of this will were very unusual in the sense that they went against established local custom whereby the first son, in this case John, inherited the family estate with various bequests then made to other members of the family. Some seven months later on April 7, 1922 the son, Marshall, who inherited the whole estate, died from heart disease and the family estate passed to Susie as his widow.

One morning in late June 1925, some four years after Chaffin Senior's death and proving of the first Will, James Pinkney, his second son, told his wife that the spirit of his father had appeared to him several times during that month in vivid dreams just before waking, standing by his bedside with a sorrowful facial expression before fading away. On one particular night his father had appeared again, this time wearing his familiar long black overcoat. He opened the overcoat and, as reported inaccurately in Mocksville's local paper the *Davie Record*, 'He pointed to the inside pocket and said, "You'll find something about my last will in my overcoat pocket". According to James Pinkney, his father actually said that 'You will find my will in my overcoat pocket' which is very different from the previous statement. Accepting that it really was his father's spirit and no ordinary dream, he went to see his mother who told him that she had given his father's old overcoat to John, the first son, who was now living in neighbouring Yadkin county some twenty miles away.

On July 6, James, accompanied by his young daughter Estelle, set off in his black Model T Ford along the bumpy drive to John's farm. They eventually found the old coat and, on examination, John's wife saw that the inside pocket lining had been hand sewn together. On cutting the stitches they found a small roll of paper tied with string, which contained not a second will but a message saying: "Read the 27th Chapter of Genesis in my daddy's old Bible" with no specific mention of any will.

Baffled, and feeling that he needed more witnesses to confirm whatever he might find next he asked his neighbour Thomas Blackwelder and Blackwelder's daughter to accompany him, his wife and Estelle to his mother's home to find the old Bible. His mother could not remember where it was and joined them as they searched the house. They eventually found it in the drawer of an unused bureau in an upstairs room. It was in such a dilapidated state that when it was picked it up it fell apart into three sections. Thomas Blackwelder happened to pick up the Old Testament section that contained the 27th Chapter of Genesis and found two facing pages that had been folded over each other to form a pocket. Inside the pocket he found a single piece of ruled, yellow tablet paper. It was a handwritten will, signed and dated by James L Chaffin that read as follows:

> After reading the 27th chapter of Genesis, I, James, L, Chaffin, do make my last will and testament, and here it is. I want, after giving my body a decent burial, my little property to be equally divided between my four children if they are living at my death, both personal and real estate, divided equal; if not living, give share to their children. And if she is still living you must all take care of your mammy. Now this is my last will and testament. Witness my hand and seal.
> Jas. L. Chaffin,
> This January 16, 1919.

In his signed statement to Mr Johnson, a North Carolina attorney who, on behalf of the Society for Psychical Research, was interviewing all concerned during 1927, Thomas Blackwelder confirmed this account by saying,

> I went with him and we made a search for the Bible and after some time we found it in a bureau drawer in the second storey of the house. We took out the Bible, which was quite old and in three pieces. I took one of the three pieces and Mr Chaffin took the other two pieces but it happened that the piece I had contained the Book of Genesis. I turned the leaves until I came to the 27th chapter, and there found two leaves folded inward, and there was a paper writing folded in these two pages which purported to be the last will of Jas. L. Chaffin.

The January 1919 date implies that this will was written fourteen years after the 1905 will and two years before the death of Chaffin Senior in 1921. Although the signature on this new will had not been independently witnessed it would still be legal under North Carolina law if, after being filed for probate, the Clerk of Davie County Superior Court accepted that the will and signature was in the handwriting of the deceased. Through their attorneys the three brothers and their mother submitted this second will for probate on July 14, 1921, signing a joint affidavit to the effect that through familiarity with their father's handwriting they were convinced that it was in the hand of James L. Chaffin, deceased. Through her attorney, Susie Chaffin issued a challenge to the legitimacy of the second will on behalf of herself and her young son. If she lost the case she would be disinherited and her son, in turn, would forfeit his first will inheritance to the whole estate and be entitled to only a quarter of its value. As the new will was now the subject of legal challenge the case was referred for trial before a judge and jury on a date set in mid-December 1925.

On the morning of the trial, with the Davie County Superior Court packed with townsfolk and reporters eager to witness a juicy family feud, the jury was duly sworn in after the usual lengthy process of rejection and selection and the judge then adjourned the case for lunch. When the court reconvened, and much to the bitter disappointment of everyone present, a lawyer announced that during the interval an 'amicable settlement' had been reached. The defendant, Susie Chaffin, now accepted that this later will was written by the deceased and had therefore withdrawn her challenge.

The following account is taken from a copy of the minutes of the judgement under Mr W. B. Snow, Judge Presiding.

> JUDGMENT BY CONSENT
> *In Re* Will of J. L. CHAFFIN *Dead*
> NORTH CAROLINA, DAVIE COUNTY. In Superior Court, *December Term, 1925.*
> During the lunch break Susie was shown the will and her two lawyers advised her that her three brothers-in-law, her mother-in-law and a Mr P. Richardson had signed an affidavit to the effect that "they were acquainted with the handwriting and signature of J. L. Chaffin having seen him write and sign his name", and "verily believed" the signature was genuine. Furthermore, they could call other friends and acquaintances to testify to this effect. Whatever her personal doubts Susie Chaffin had no way of refuting their united opinion. Realising that she would lose the case she withdrew her challenge and declared the will

> genuine. In return, the brothers offered to pay one thousand dollars to her son as compensation for his reduced expectations from the estate.

Her public acceptance that the second will and signature was in the handwriting of the deceased and the jury's verdict to that effect became national news. 'Dead Man returns in Dream' ran one local headline. 'Can the Dead speak from the Grave?' asked another.

From my other researches the answer to the last question seems to be, 'Yes, the dead definitely can'. However, back to this case.

The court's decision ensured wide publicity in America and in Britain. In 1926 the Society for Psychical Research (SPR) engaged Mr J. M. N. Johnson to review the case and obtain signed statements from the main participants. In April 1927 he commenced his inquiry as a complete sceptic but became so impressed with the apparent honesty of all involved that in his report to Mr Salter, then secretary of the SPR he said, 'I believe I am safe in asserting that if you once talked with these honest people and looked into their clear, unsophisticated countenances, your criticism would vanish into thin air as mine did'. They were, he said, all "honest, honourable country people, in well-to-do circumstances". Mr Johnson concluded that however improbable the story might seem, his father's spirit really had visited James Pinkney for the purpose of revealing the whereabouts of a second will, written and signed by himself.

Mr W. H. Salter, honorary secretary of the SPR at the time, was also a practising barrister-at-law and his legal experience had made him somewhat cynical of human motives. As a seasoned investigator of alleged ghostly phenomena who later wrote a book on ghosts, he remained singularly unconvinced. In his reply to Mr Johnson he pointed out some puzzling features of the case. If, he said, Chaffin Senior had changed his mind, why not just see his attorney and draft a new will? Why write it on a piece of paper and hide it in the dilapidated, no longer used Bible that had belonged to his father? Why write a separate note saying to read the 27th chapter of Genesis without any explanation as to why? Why put the rolled-up note in his inside overcoat pocket and then sew the pocket up? Also, why didn't Chaffin Senior's spirit just tell James Pinkney that the will was in "His daddie's old bible"? After all, he would have known where it was if he had put it there. Again, why wait four years?

None of this made any sense to Mr Salter at all. After all, as he pointed out, if they had thrown away his old overcoat because no one wanted it, and thrown out the disintegrating old Bible as well, the will would never have been found. Salter, obviously unimpressed by anyone's 'clear, unsophisticated countenances' after many years in court ended his very sceptical reply to Mr Johnson in true barrister language, saying, "There is, I admit, no limit to the folly of testators or the secretiveness of farmers, but the present testator seems to have pushed both these characteristics to the extreme. But for the apparition, his testamentary wishes would never have been carried out, and one can hardly suppose that during his life he counted upon being able to appear as a ghost".

One for Salter I feel.

Mr Johnson replied, sticking firmly to his conclusions suggested the following scenario based upon hints dropped by a neighbour concerning the Chaffins. Gossip had it that Chaffin Senior "lived in mortal fear" of his daughter-in-law Susie who, the neighbour thought, knew about the 1905 will in their favour. Unwilling to face her he hid his new will, thinking that he would tell his sons where it was when he was dying, but died before telling them. Now living in spirit and full of remorse at the injustice delivered by his original will, he decided that the only way he could inform them about the second will was to appear to James Pinkney in his dreams, show him the inside pocket of the overcoat and tell him, very inaccurately as it turned out, what was in it. As Mr Johnson saw it, "This man J. P. Chaffin is an honest man and he thoroughly believes his father's spirit appeared to him and gave him the clue to the 1919 will". Salter, however, remained unconvinced, suggesting an alternative scenario in which John, or maybe Abner, faked the will, put it into the old Bible and then wrote the note, which he stitched into the overcoat pocket. He absolved James Pinkney of lying by suggesting that he had acted as an innocent go-between, fooled into thinking that he'd seen and heard his father's spirit when, in fact, it was John who had quietly let himself into the bedroom dressed in the old overcoat, murmured those words in James Pinkney's ear, and crept out again. This now sounds like a soap opera, but bear with me.

There the matter rested as far as a very sceptical secretary of the SPR was concerned. But, for the public at large and believers in life after death in particular, the story had taken on a life of its own. Authors of books and articles on ghosts, apparitions and life after death communications included it as a legally validated case of post-mortem visitation by a father to his son to redress the balance of inheritance that he had got so badly wrong in his first will. For example, Hilary Evans, an experienced investigator of ghosts and apparitions, accepted it as well-validated evidence for post mortem survival saying, "The famous Chaffin Will case, because legal issues were involved, is fully documented with affidavits from everyone involved, so the facts are not in dispute". The late Colin Wilson judged the case as offering "One of the strongest pieces of evidence for survival after death". Professor David Fontana, another experienced investigator of psychical phenomena, quotes the Chaffin case as one of the best-known examples "of apparitions who supply accurate information unknown to witnesses" and refers readers to Berger for a full account and legal opinion. Berger, a retired attorney who had been an instructor in law and a municipal attorney, concluded that the verdict of the court was the right one. By 1938 even Salter had come to the reluctant conclusion that the will was genuine. It was, he said, either a case of "A supernormal agency of some kind" or, as some had suggested, James Pinkney had known of the second will but had forgotten about it until a "latent memory had revived some years later and 'externalised itself' in the form of repeated bedside visions". Given the four-year interval between his father's death and the dream, he felt that the latter explanation was frankly untenable leaving a 'supernormal agency' as the most likely explanation. What all these commentators are agreed upon is that the second will was indeed written and signed by James. L. Chaffin and its previously unknown existence was revealed by his spirit appearing in his son's dreams just prior to waking.

Despite unanimity of opinion as to its validity the question remains: *was the second will written and signed by the deceased?* At the trial, testimony as to its authenticity rested solely upon the opinion of family and friends acquainted with his handwriting. Susie Chaffin's withdrawal of her challenge in the face of this united opinion did not prove its authenticity, nor did the verdict of the jury as their verdict of 'Yes' had become a matter of legal formality concerning a document that they never examined once she had withdrawn her legal challenge and all the litigants seemed agreed.

Mary Roach, a well-known American investigative reporter and author who was writing a book on the evidence offered by believers for life after death, tackled this question directly. In April 2004 she visited Mocksville to talk to James Pinkny's two elderly grandsons, Lester and Lloyd, in an attempt to discover what stories had been handed down through the family. Both remained convinced that their grandfather really had been visited by his father's spirit who wished to redress a wrong and direct him to the second will. When Lester was a teenager James Pinkney used to tell him the story of the dream and what happened afterwards. His mother Estelle had described their dusty and rackety journey to John's house and their eventual discovery of the grubby old overcoat with its sewn up inside pocket and covered in 'dirt dobber' (old wasp nests). They dismissed Salter's theory that John had impersonated a ghost on the basis that, "like Pink, John didn't talk much, didn't go for foolishness". As for James Pinkney making it up, "Pink would never have thought of that" said Lester. "Nope," said Lloyd, "He would have considered that crooked". They described their grandfather as an honest, practical, Baptist church-going farmer who worked long hours and was not known for any form of psychical experience except for this one.

I am reminded of the old saying, 'Where there is a will there is a family'.

Was the second will in Chaffin Senior's handwriting?

I leave you to decide.

**Fig 1. Comparison between the signatures of James L Chaffin as written in the 1905 first Will (top) and the 1919 second Will (bottom). Enlarged.**

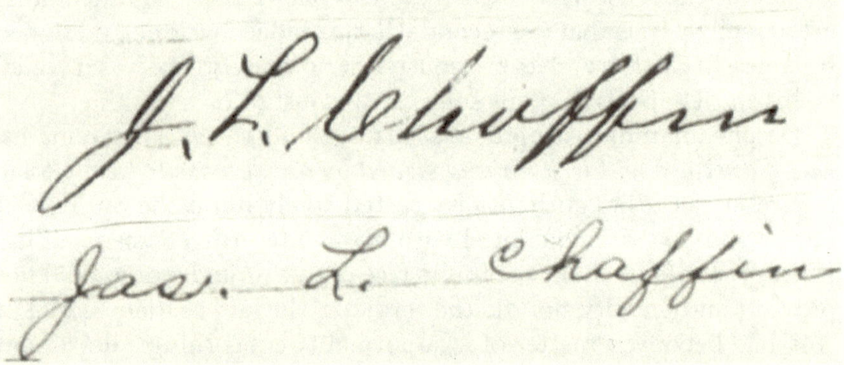

We will never know for certain, but a court obviously thought it plausible that a discarnate being was able to provide such information and that is *very* interesting in itself.

**References**

1. Salter W. H. (1928). Case of the Will of James, L, Chaffin. Proceedings of the Society for Psychical Research. Vol. XXXV1 p 517-24.

2. Oaten, E.W. (1928). *The Chaffin Will Case.* Manchester: Two Worlds Publishing Co.

# 7

## Do Healing Miracles Happen?

It is widely accepted that people can enjoy very positive results from, what may be called, spiritual healing in its various forms. Indeed I have studied and researched this topic for five years myself and have concluded via the evidence gathered that an improvement in health conditions can certainly be achieved. At this point it would be useful to expand on the healing phenomenon.

There are different categories of healing. Absent or distant healing, akin to prayer where directed *intention* is in some way projected to help the recipient make a recovery.

Hands-on-healing, which involves the laying on of hands, either on or just above the patient. This can be done within the theology of any particular religion, or out-with any religious context.

Psychic surgery – this involves healing which appears to produce a surgical outcome on the patient. This has been demonstrated both with and without the use of surgical implements.

Throughout the recent decades many absent healing studies have been carefully carried out and they have provided very interesting results.

Randolph Byrd, M.D. ran a well controlled study using prayer and/or distant healing which was, by thought, sent to 192 cardiac patients, while another 201 similar patients acted as a control group. The control group were not sent any healing intentions at all, neither by prayer or any other means.

All of the patients knew that they were taking part in an experiment and that they would be randomly assigned to one of the groups. They were not told which of the groups they were in and, as no significant differences were noted on many variables, comparisons were fair.

The results showed very clearly that the patients who were 'thought about' recovered significantly quicker than those in the control group.

Daniel J. Benor, M.D. in the year 2000 reviewed sixty-one reports of distant (absent) healing studies. I find it most interesting that he found that the distance between the person sending the healing thoughts and the recipient did not appear to affect the outcome. By that I mean that thoughts sent to someone in another country were just as effective as those sent to someone in the same city as the sender. He also noted that there was no data to support the idea that healing in a religious context is any more efficacious than outside a religious context.

Dr Benor was a traditional medical doctor until 1980. As a psychiatrist, he initially thought that healing was no more than wishful thinking or charlatanism. He then witnessed a healing, which produced an amazing result within half an hour and he, as a sensible open-minded person, began to examine the phenomenon for himself.

There have been more than 180 scientific studies regarding forms of spiritual healing and more than half of these show highly significant effects against the positive results being due to chance. The following is but one example.

For those of you with no interest in maths, just read the bottom line and know that the smaller the end number and more zeros there are *after* the point, the more significant the result is.

Astin, Ernst and Harkness reviewed twenty-three studies: five with prayer, eleven with non-contact healing and seven with other miscellaneous distant healing approaches. The overall results for sixteen double-blind trials in each category produced the following results.

For prayer the p value (probability due to chance) was 0.0009

For distant healing by intention the p value was 0.0003

These are highly significant results as 0.05 in science suggests that future experiments in any field should be carried out.

There have been many outstanding healers of the past, one being the well-known Harry Edwards who died in 1976. He was a contact healer who was involved with a spiritual healing sanctuary in Burrows Lea, Surrey for over forty years.

During this time he wrote many books including "The Evidence for Spirit Healing" in which he cites literally thousands of cases, supported by medical data.

One quote suggests that, "Even sceptics will find their conception of the impossible narrowed by the astonishing facts in this book".

Reports of his outstanding healing successes were very well authenticated and highly significant over those forty years.

The journalist Beverly Nichols, initially sceptical, also eventually stated that he was impressed and convinced by his work.

Seemingly miraculous healings could take place instantly, even to laying his hands on a goitre, which disappeared instantly. Or stroking the very bent back of an elderly woman who had this condition for a number of years – and as he did so she was able to straighten up and maintain that position.

Now we come to the word miracle. Definitions of 'miracle' vary in every dictionary, but they invariably ascribe a miracle to God, or some other name for a deity.

With regard to healing they also state that a 'miracle' is something, 'Exhibiting control over the laws of nature and serving as evidence that the agent is either divine or is specially favoured by God'.

This would not be my definition, but simply an occurrence, which cannot be explained within the understanding and parameters of science AS WE KNOW IT at this time.

Knowledge grows as mankind grows and ideas change as new information comes to light. As an example, Newtonian physicists would have been aghast at the theories of Quantum physics ... 'nonsense!' they would have said, but the world now accepts quantum theory.

Now let us consider psychic surgery.

For many years there have been claims that people can heal others by means of psychic surgery. Some operations appear to be non-invasive and take place within the body of the patient but others appear to employ actual surgery where a scar or opening is evident.

As in every other area of life there will be frauds, or people who exaggerate their abilities, but I will concentrate on three absolutely genuine exponents who have stood the test of time, the first being a gentleman by the name of Arigo.

## *Arigo*

He was from Brazil and came to be known as the 'Surgeon of the Rusty Knife'. You will understand why in a little while. It is important to remember that he sought no fame and took no payment for his work.

He was a very active trade unionist who represented miners; a man of the people with aspirations of being a politician.

Arigo was in his early 40s and looked like a truck driver, burly and normal, with little time for the 'graces' in life. However, he discovered as he matured that he could heal people, an ability that developed into psychic surgery in which he often used the aid of a knife, any knife, to effect a physical cure. Along with this he developed the skill of being able to write an individualised prescription for a patient; a prescription, which was tailored and effective for only that one person. By this I mean that two people who had the same condition would not necessarily receive the same prescription.

He had no medical training at all.

On hearing of his claimed abilities, a well known respected American psychical researcher Dr Andrija Puharich brought a team of researchers to attend a healing session by Arigo.

Many colour films of Arigo's operations had already been recorded, Puharich and his team also brought recording equipment with them.

By 7:00 a.m. there were nearly two hundred people in the streets as the doors of this strange clinic were opened. Arigo gave his spare time to his healing work, which was mostly at weekends. Word had somehow got around that Puharich's research team had arrived –although they had not announced it. On arrival, the team were unceremoniously waved ahead of the actual patients.

As they entered they noted that written on a crumpled brown piece of paper on the rickety wall was, "Don't lean against the wall – think of Jesus".

I think that I am the only person in the world who actually finds that humorous.

The meeting started in prayer and then Arigo retired to a cubicle. When he reappeared he seemed like a different person, his eyes were radiantly piercing but somehow looked out of focus.

He invited the researchers to stand by the table that he would be working at, stating, "I have nothing to hide".

The first patient in the line was an elderly, well-dressed man. Without any warning Arigo suddenly grabbed him and held him against the wall and then without uttering a word he picked up a 4-inch stainless-steel paring knife and literally plunged it into the man's eye, under the lid and deep up into the eye socket.

In spite of his medical experience Puharich was shocked and stunned, even more so when Arigo began scraping the knife between the ocular globe and under the inside of the lid.

The man was wide awake, fully conscious and showed no discomfort or fear whatsoever.

He did not flinch throughout the whole procedure. During the 'scraping' a woman in the background screamed and another fainted.

Arigo then levered the eye out so that it extruded from the socket and lay partially on the patient's cheek.

While all of this was going on the patient seemed more bothered about a fly that had landed on his other cheek as he nonchalantly tried several times to brush the fly away with his hand.

After the eye had been returned to the socket Arigo turned away leaving the knife partially in the man's eye. He then asked Puharich to place his finger on the eyelid so that he could feel the knife under the skin. By this time Puharich was almost in a state of shock and Henry Belk, another experienced researcher who was with him, also felt limp and nauseated.

Arigo then dismissed the patient saying, "You will be well".

The whole procedure had taken less than a minute.

The researchers and other onlookers watched patient after patient getting "treatment".

It actually appeared to the researchers that Arigo could stem blood flow with almost a command. He would say things like, 'Jesus wants you to stop bleeding,' and patients did stop bleeding. I admit that perhaps it was a psychosomatic reaction, but it worked.

That evening Puharich was lying in his bed scratching his arm when he thought of a personal test for Arigo. He had a fatty lipoma on his arm, which was not really dangerous, but to remove it could cause complications as it was near a group of nerves. The position of this lipoma meant that an operation could possibly result in the restriction of the movement in his fingers or, worse still, damage the ulna nerve. For this reason Western doctors were not keen to touch it.

As Puharich deliberated his position he realised that he was not too keen on the fact that there would be no anaesthetic, but eventually decided that for proof one way or the other he would let Arigo operate on his lipoma.

When he presented himself for surgery the next day Arigo seemed amused and joked with the crowd as he said, "Has anybody here got a good Brazilian knife to use on the Americano?" Immediately half-a-dozen pocket-knives were held high and offered with laughter in an almost carnival like atmosphere.

I am not sure that Pucharich would be smiling at that point.

Researcher Belk had his Polaroid camera at the ready; Rizzini had a 6mm film camera ready for action and poor Puharich was most probably very apprehensive.

Arigo said, "We will do the arm". Things were now moving so quickly that the research team rushed to check that the cameras were set up properly.

Arigo instructed Puharich to look away; as he did so he checked the lighting and the cameras.

Ten seconds later Puharich felt something wet in his hand, it was his lipoma. On his arm was a small slit with a trickle of blood dripping down from it. He was stunned – he had not felt anything at all. As his brain engaged he began to worry as he thought of another factor to consider. Arigo had not washed or disinfected either the knife or his skin. Septicaemia was a distinct possibility under these conditions. However he managed to calm himself down as he reasoned that if the wound healed cleanly it would be another exhibition of Arigo's powers.

The session continued.

One of the other patients after Puharich was a man with a very large fluid laden testicle.

The patient stood there calmly as Arigo stabbed a knife into it and drew off some fluid into an orange drink bottle. When that was full he then used a coke bottle to collect the remaining liquid. The man appeared to feel no pain. Arigo then said to him, 'Now you can go and get married'.

During his time as a healer and psychic surgeon, the medical associations in Brazil were very much opposed to Arigo's practises.

The Roman Catholic Church was also none too happy about him.

Arigo was expecting legal action to be taken against him at any time and that eventually took place. When he was placed in jail for a short time his cell door was never locked and he was given free range and encouraged to give people healing where necessary.

Where the acclaimed healer George Chapman had Mr Lang, a consultant ophthalmologist, as his discarnate psychic surgeon, Arigo said that it was a German Doctor Fritz who worked through him.

The difference being that from the amount of information given to Chapman by Lang, Mr Lang was indeed successfully identified as a genuine consultant from Moorfields hospital, but Dr Fritz's identity never was really verified.

So what was the outcome of the lipoma operation?

Puharich suffered NO infection, along with every other patient treated.

We will come back to this point later.

About thirteen years before Arigo recognised his own surgical "talents" he attended a particular Union meeting. Among the attendees was a Senator Bittencourt who was also very interested in the rights of the ordinary working man and he liked Arigo's ideas. After the meeting he invited Arigo to stay overnight in an upmarket hotel, so that they could talk.

Now, unknown to anyone at the meeting, Bittencourt had a lung cancer and his only hope was to undergo an operation. After retiring from a productive evening in conversation with Arigo, Bittencourt awaked in the middle of the night to find Arigo in his room, standing over him holding an open razor in his outstretched hand. He also noted that Arigo had a glazed look in his eyes just before he passed out and awakened at 5:00 a.m. to find himself wearing blood stained pyjamas.

When Bittencourt subsequently visited his own surgeon for a check up in hospital the doctor said, "Oh I see that you have had the operation". I have no idea as to how he answered that statement.

Incidentally, when Arigo was later shown a film of himself operating on a patient he fainted at the sight of blood.

A more comprehensive account of Arigo's work can be found in the book *Arigo, Surgeon of the Rusty Knife.* In this book you can see a photo of the tiny cut in Puharich's arm with a trickle of blood running down from it. There is no dubiety about this whole event.

There are also many genuine psychic surgeons described in a wonderful book by Guy Lyon Playfair, *The Unknown Power* and I will give you a flavour of two of them. Firstly a man named Antonio Sales.

*The Unknown Power* was later revised and released under the title, *The Flying Cow.*

## *Antonio Sales*

He developed his mediumistic skills around 1949 and became known as the quiet man of psychic surgery. He always wore a white coat and kept everything clean, neat and tidy. Former patients of his told Guy that he was a calm and friendly man who spoke kindly to them.

One woman said that he was just like any other doctor whereas in her opinion, 'Arigo was very crude indeed'. It is my understanding that Sales also did not charge for his healing.

However the two healers had one thing in common: a spirit healer by the name of Dr Fritz. One may view this with some scepticism as by this time Arigo had passed over and many people were claiming that Dr Fritz worked with them. Maybe he did work with other people, no one really knows, but in one particular case a previous patient of Arigo, who had been prescribed pills for inflammation of the ovaries, attended Sales for a different problem. When her consultation with Sales began, a thick Germanic voice said to her, 'Ah, I am glad you took those pills' and mentioned them by name. Apart from the correct information about the pills it sounded to her very much like the same Dr Fritz. I find that very interesting, as the specific name of a pill would not be easy to guess.

Another witness related to Guy Playfair a description of how Sales treated a girl with tonsillitis.

> 'He thrust a pair of scissors into her mouth and started cutting away, telling the girl not to worry because everything was sterilised. I noticed the smell of ether around the place but saw no sign of anybody sterilising anything at all'. This perceived smell of ether has also been noted with other healers.
>
> I saw something like this myself in a private video that I have in my possession where John of God stuck scissors up one man's nose in not too gentle a fashion and then another where he thrust something that looked like a scalpel into another man's ear. There appeared to be no mention of sterilisation of equipment. Both patients did not seem to feel pain but I have to say that they looked a bit stunned and 'out of it'. It is the kind of scenario that you watch with one eye closed.

Back to Sales. Another woman related to Guy, 'Before I went to Sales, I had to wear gloves. My arms and hands were simply hideous with a sort of rash that nobody could cure – look at my hands now, aren't they beautiful?' It is my understanding that this betterment continued.

However around 1971 Sales appeared to lose his healing gifts. There was some concern that his own church and the medical profession were harassing him and that this emotional instability took its toll.

I included this healer chiefly because of the ostensible link with the elusive Dr Fritz.

And now a second example from Guy's book, a gentleman named Edivaldo.

## *Edivaldo*

Just like Arigo and Sales, Edivaldo took NO payment whatsoever; he believed in Jesus and he gave nearly all of his spare time to helping other people. He had a casual manner, almost appearing indifferent at times.

Guy Lyon Playfair spent a full two years in Brazil investigating claims of genuine psychic surgery. With a view to interviewing Edivaldo, Guy visited the appointed healing venue. Surprisingly the waiting room proved to be very run down and rickety. This healer's dedication could not be challenged as he held surgery every weekend without fail and he would have to travel five hundred miles to get there.

Edivaldo was a well-educated and very intelligent man, aged about forty and of slight build. This gave him a completely different appearance from the burlier Arigo.

During his interview with Guy, Edivaldo said that he has several "attending spirits" and that he never asked for them, they just came. He explained that he withdraws his spirit and usually a Dr Calazans takes over, adding the rider that, 'There isn't room for two spirits in the one body, you see!' He also said that when he withdraws his spirit all that he feels is a strong light in his eyes which is like that of a welder's blowlamp, and then he is 'out'.

His other spirit helpers included a Frenchman called Dr Pierre, a Londoner called Johnson, a Dr Fritz from Germany, a Japanese man, an Italian and a Brazilian.

Guy then attended a public healing session. He watched Edivaldo run a finger down the belly of a male patient and witnessed the skin parting, showing some intestines. When the surgery was finished he ran a finger up the opening and the skin sealed itself. If you think that Guy was too far away to see properly you would be wrong, he was standing beside Edivaldo while he 'operated'. Based on this experience Guy asked if he could be seen as a patient. At that point he told Guy that he needed a small operation and to come back at another time. He did come back many weeks later.

When he did Guy said, "It's my digestion Doctor". The somewhat terse reply, presumably from Dr Calazans, was, "I know, that's where I'm looking" as he scribbled a prescription for him at the same time. Both Arigo and Edivaldo had the ability to write specific prescriptions individualised to each patient, as did the well-known Chico Xavier. As mentioned earlier, I mean that if two people had the same condition they would not necessarily receive the same prescriptive medication.

Guy was then given an operation, which left a small scar and two stitch marks each side on his body. The scar disappeared fairly quickly, but there was some evidence of the "dots" from the stitch marks throughout his life. He only noticed the scar and dots in a mirror the day after the procedure. However, immediately after the operation Guy felt quite ill and had to be taken to lie down in another room. Edivaldo came to see him and asked whom he had brought along with him. When he heard that Guy was alone he laughed sarcastically and muttered something along the lines of, 'He has an operation and thinks he needs no one to help him; this is an operation like any other; you need to take care'.

The result was an improvement in Guy's digestion, which was now better than it had been for many years.

After that, Guy was granted a private interview with the healer. This was in the early 1970s. At that time, he told Guy that in ten years of performing these healings he estimated that he had treated 65,000 clients. Guy had assumed that Edivaldo was a Spiritist but was told in no uncertain manner that he was a Christian who tried to love his neighbour and do what he could do to help people. When Guy mentioned parapsychology and psychical research Edivaldo was slightly dismissive, showed little interest and said, 'They only study the soul; mediumship shows what the soul can do'.

In Scotland we would say, "that was him told"!

In case you are confused, healing can be considered as a part of mediumship.

Guy was subsequently invited to attend a healing session at a different venue, a much smaller and cleaner one. The room was full and Guy was near the door. The proceedings began with Dr Pierre speaking in French followed by others in English, Italian and German. Then Dr

Calazans, the MC for the evening, entered and announced that he represented all of the others. He spoke in Spanish throughout, which was fortunate as Guy was fluent in that language. Calazans suddenly called out for the 'ingles' to come to the front. He was greeted by, 'So you're the parapsychologist, are you? – take a chair and come and sit by me'. He then said, 'Where is your tape recorder? Guy replied that he did not have it with him. 'Go fetch it. I suppose you would go fishing without a fishing rod!' To be fair to Guy he had left it outside, as he did not want to assume that he would be allowed to use it. Guy dutifully, and no doubt somewhat sheepishly, returned with the tape recorder.

Calazans then stood over a patient, a Brazilian man around 30 years old who was lying down on a bed with his bare stomach in view. He waved his hands around and spoke as if giving a lecture to students explaining the parts of the innards. He broke off to ask Guy if he could see properly. Guy replied that indeed he could. The next question was, 'With the eyes, or with the mind? ... reply ...'Er, with the eyes at least'.... Calazans seemed highly amused.

The patient was asked how he felt and the response was a grunt.

Calazan's turned to Guy and said, 'Now he is feeling it open – not in the mind but in the body itself, above the stomach'. Guy then heard a commentary of what was supposed to be taking place within the man's stomach area. There was nothing physical to be seen. When he was finished someone asked how long the man should rest. Forty-eight hours was the reply. It transpired that this man was also attending alone and when he asked if he could drive himself home Calazans, once again, seemed amused as he retorted, 'Only if you go by rocket; next patient please!'

And so it continued. He then told Guy that the next operation would be a physical one. The patient was an attractive young woman; she lay down on the bed and again bared her stomach area. Guy could see Calazans prodding around the woman's stomach when he commanded Guy to do the same. The area seemed wet although Guy couldn't really see anything. Suddenly Calazans rubbed a finger on her skin and almost stuck it up Guy's nose. The smell of ether was unmistakable. The woman seemed unperturbed. Guy put his hand on a small part of her stomach. Calazans began the operation and it was indeed messy; after a few twists and wrenches, his hands were immersed in a pool of dark liquid that had appeared from nowhere.

'Go On' Calazans insisted, 'Put your hand in!' Guy managed to put one finger into the liquid to a depth of around one inch. It was warm and looked lighter and thinner than blood. Then Guy remembered that Calazans had been speaking earlier about separating red corpuscles from plasma. 'Oxygenated water!' Calazans ordered, and an assistant poured some liquid from a small bottle onto the woman's stomach. As it frothed and bubbled Guy snatched his finger away. As he did so the liquid pool on the woman's stomach simply vanished, like spilt water in a cartoon. Calazans said, 'How would you do that by parapsychology, eh?'

Calazans also seemed to be able to diagnose instantly. Guy had surreptitiously brought along with him a girl with ear trouble. Calazans had not even looked at her but handed her a written prescription for her ear problem.

This healer then continued with patient after patient, addressing various ailments.

When the session was over, Guy wrote, 'I was in the position of an ancient Greek rubbing two pieces of amber together and producing what would be known as electricity nearly two thousand years later, without having any idea of what he was doing'.

When he returned to his accommodation, Guy poured a cold beer and tried to make some kind of sense out of the evening's events. He turned to Einstein for help and read the following: 'To know that what is impenetrable to us really exists, manifesting itself as the highest wisdom and the most radiant beauty which our dull faculties can comprehend only in their most primitive forms – this knowledge, this feeling is the centre of true religiousness'.

Guy finished his beer and wrote the following, 'It was good to know that some things were impenetrable even to Einstein. They certainly were to me'.

I knew Guy reasonable well and adored his laconic sense of humour.

By the time Edivaldo had come to prominence, Arigo had been killed in a car crash, but, if you cast your mind back to my earlier text, he too had a 'surgeon' called Dr Fritz. Yes, it appears that it is he again. I wonder if it was indeed the same person who then attached himself to Sales' and Arigo's work. This is pure speculation of course and has no proof, but I think worth a thought.

As with Arigo and Sales, Edivaldo's patients again felt no fear and they had little discomfort although no actual physical anaesthetic was used.

To the best of my knowledge, in over forty years of researchers studying the combined work of psychic surgeons, NO infections whatsoever have been reported from patients regarding any of these procedures, both from those people already mentioned and other genuine psychic surgeons.

Guy actually asked Edivaldo if he had ever had a case of post op infection. He laughed his head off and said, 'If I had, you would have heard about it!'

It is worth noting that some other patients had an appropriate surgical scar in the area of the operation, whether or not an instrument was used. This would tie in with The Chapman/Lang surgery where Mr. Lang explained that he operated on the patient's etheric body and this then had a corresponding effect on the physical body.

We now have to consider whether the operations that I have described were carried out by the physically living person or IS there another factor to consider?

Is it feasible that the surgeons discussed are indeed "taken over" in a temporary capacity by a competent deceased personality, with all of the medical knowledge and skills of that person? That is certainly one explanation, which fits the facts.

This may be your boggle factor limit – but you must weigh up the wealth of evidence in detail before discarding this hypothesis, or provide another competing theory that fits ALL of the facts.

In as much as we cannot understand the methodology of inexplicable successful healing, I contend that, even now in this age of technology, 'Healing miracles do happen!'

# 8

## The Man Of The Unholy Cross

This account is derived from actual case notes relating to psychotherapy sessions and the first hand experiences of Professor Archie Roy, who was a Professor of Astronomy at the University of Glasgow.

Before he passed, Archie gave me the relevant psychotherapist's case notes with instructions that I should make this case public. Due to its contents I had put it on the back burner for a few years in case of possible identification issues.

However, all but one of the people involved has now passed on, making actual identification of the subject less likely.

In a strange way I became involved in this case at a later date but not in a way that you might guess.

In the mid 1980s Professor Roy received a telephone call from a psychotherapist who was puzzled by the responses of a female client. The woman in her thirties had come for treatment for various stress-related issues and disturbing dreams. This psychotherapist had been practising very successfully for many years and sometimes, where appropriate, she would employ hypnosis as part of her treatment.

I will call this client Julie, not her real name of course. I will call the psychotherapist Anne, also not her real name.

Anne informed Archie that after several sessions with her client Julie began speaking in a foreign language when she was in a hypnotic state. Anne thought that it sounded like German. She had never come across this before. Neither woman had any knowledge of German in their ordinary lives. Archie Roy possessed a smattering of German and therefore, with everyone's permission, arrangements were made for him to attend a psychotherapy session.

As a child Julie had nightmarish recurring dreams about war, death and destruction, which left her almost constantly fearful. Her family were very puzzled since she had no experience of such events, unless maybe from something that she might have seen on television, but they felt that most unlikely.

At the first session that Archie attended he could verify that the odd foreign word that she uttered was indeed German. During future sessions he would try to ask her simple questions in German when she was in the hypnotic state.

At each subsequent session her ability to speak German became clearer and more fluent, until one day it became clear to Archie that the recurring dreams that she was describing fitted events eerily similar to an assassination attempt on the life of Obergruppenfuhrer Reinhard Heydrich.

Under hypnosis she became agitated as she described travelling in an open-top car, nearing a hairpin bend, seeing a man standing with one arm slightly hidden under a coat, and as 'she' passed in the car this man produced a gun, pointed it at 'her' and pulled the trigger. However the gun jammed and 'she' was then able to produce a gun and shoot at the man.

In actual fact this was indeed a very clear description that fitted the conditions of an attempted assassination on Heydrich's life. He did pass along a particular road on a regular basis and his driver always had to drastically slow down his Mercedes to take a hairpin bend, making it an ideal place for an assassination attempt. The man holding the gun was a Czech by the name of Gabcik and part of a team who were hell bent on killing this 'butcher'. The gun that he used was a British Sten gun and, as already described, as Gabcik pulled the trigger, the gun jammed leaving a second member of his team, Kubis, to throw a grenade into the car. The gun's jamming allowed Heydrich time to draw a gun and shoot back at Gabcik.

Under hypnosis Julie described this scenario to perfection and added that 'she' was then taken to a nearby hospital in a baker's van. Archie assured me that this was subsequently shown to be correct although I cannot personally verify it.

Apparently, Heydrich, then 38 years old, suffered serious injuries in the attack and died eight days later, on June 4, 1942.

Heydrich was known as the Butcher of Berlin. He was cruel and ruthless. His official description was as follows.

Reinhard Tristan Eugen Heydrich was a high-ranking German Nazi official during World War II, and a main architect of the Holocaust.

He was an SS-Obergruppenführer und General der Polizei as well as chief of the Reich Main

Security Office. He was also Stellvertretender Reichsprotektor of Bohemia and Moravia.

He also served as president of the International Criminal Police Commission and chaired the January 1942 Wannsee Conference, which formalised plans for the Final Solution to the Jewish 'problem' as they saw it.

As the psychotherapist sessions progressed, the Heydrich personality became stronger and stronger until it got to a point where Julie could sit up and hold a conversation with Archie. 'She' was unrelenting regarding the life of Heydrich. Archie would prod her shoulder and say things like, 'Do you not know that you are not doing yourself any good by affecting this girl in this way?' The reply was that he did not care.

'He' could sing German songs relating to the war and constantly referred to the motto above the concentration camps, *Arbeit macht frei*. The translation of this being 'Work sets one free'.

Heydrich boasted to Archie about his social interactions with Hitler and other major players in the SS. He spoke about playing sport with them and gave specific details regarding days and times when these events took place. Although there was no sign of remorse or any such emotion regarding his time as "the butcher" it became clear that he did love his wife and children. 'His' voice softened when he spoke about them. Archie tried to appeal to this situation and suggested that if Heydrich left this girl alone he could go forward and be reunited with his wife and children. This also fell on stony ground.

As the months passed, Archie and the psychotherapist were eventually told by him that, 'When Julie was a little girl I could see her sitting in her garden. As she got older I could then see the garden through her eyes. Eventually her eyes became mine'.

Now, using the analogy of a car, he continued, 'Julie used to drive the car and I sat in the back seat, now I drive the car and she is in the back seat'.

This sounds somewhat creepy and scary, and indeed it is.

In her everyday life, Julie gradually adopted a male-like persona. She had her hair cut in a very short style, wore long knee boots, a leather jacket and a cap of sorts, resembling a military style. She even bought an old open-topped car and had a relevant number plate made for it; one with a strong link to Heydrich and the SS.

Archie then took a respite from attending the psychotherapist's sessions and it was nearly a year into this case when he received a telephone call at Glasgow University, which at first left him perplexed. He couldn't understand who was on the line. Now speaking in English the voice said, 'Its Reiny, Reiny-Reinhard Heydrich'. After Archie's initial shock they had a conversation, which ended with Archie agreeing to meet 'him' for a drink.

On the day of the meeting Archie, a fully self-confessed member of the coward's club, began to worry as he thought to himself, 'You are mad, Roy, Heydrich used to poison people!'

However he did meet 'him;' they chatted over a drink and he lived to tell the tale. Archie noted that Heydrich's attitudes seemed somewhat softer than before, but he still had no intentions whatever of moving on. And to date that is the way that it has been left as far as I know.

Now, an addendum to this case.

About ten years after these events and making no reference to them, Archie said to me, 'I need a reading with a good medium very soon, and I am not going to tell you why'. Naturally I said OK, as I knew better than to question Archie, since he would never have asked unless it was important.

At that time I lived alone and I invited Archie and a medium to my flat where we could conduct this reading and have dinner. For the sake of accuracy I decided to record the sitting on a cassette recorder.

The medium knew as much as I did about the purpose of the evening: i.e. nothing, only that Professor Roy would like a reading.

Everyone agreed that the reading should be held first followed by wine and dinner.

Archie and the medium sat on individual couches opposite each other about seven feet apart; I sat in silence on an individual chair ready to operate the tape recorder and I kept as far away from them as possible, just in case that I would in some way interfere with this mystery reading.

And so it began. The medium, who was looking intently at Archie the whole time, started by saying, 'I feel a choking, like smoke; it is catching my throat'. This gave me no clue so far as to the purpose of the meeting. The medium seemed to be confused and repeated about the smoke while touching her throat. I noticed that she seemed to be very slowly drawn back into the high headrest of the couch as her eyes slowly closed. Archie and I sat in silence just staring at her. I don't think that we even looked at each other. The medium then leaned forward and slowly stood up, adopting an 'air' completely different from that of before. Her eyes were closed and remained closed throughout the whole subsequent twenty-minute session. She initially turned her head towards me and said, 'Good evening madam', and then gave me personal information about future events, which subsequently came true: events that I had no control over. She then turned to Archie and said very clearly and concisely, 'I have had to come this evening as my medium speaks such nonsense'. I remember thinking, 'Oh what's this, that will not go down well, or something along these lines'.

She then said, 'You wish to speak of the man of the unholy cross'. I then realised that this must be something to do with the Heydrich events from all these years ago. It took me a few moments to realise that she was speaking about the swastika as being the unholy cross.

For around 20 minutes she spoke of the events around Julie, and expounded a dissertation as to why possession was not possible in this case. She described 'the man of the unholy cross' as a stain on the girl's consciousness as it was not possible for two personalities to inhabit a body at the same time. She (the medium) never actually mentioned Julie by name.

Her delivery was completely different from that of the medium in accent, grammar and syntax. The content was of a very high grammatical standard throughout the whole session. Not one word was wasted. It had an air of authority. She never hesitated or faltered in any way while putting forward her views; it was flawless. When she was finished, eyes still closed, she sat slowly back on the couch and rested for a few moments with her head resting once again on the high back. I did not know that this medium could go into trance and I am sure that Archie was stunned as well. We sat in complete silence and once again I don't think that we even looked at each other since we were focused on her. On returning to normal consciousness the medium remembered nothing of the dialogue.

Not much was said then except thank you and we had dinner and a good chat about ordinary matters.

I was still bewildered as to why Archie wanted a reading at that time. It later transpired that he had seen an article in a newspaper announcing the death of the psychotherapist, Anne, who had been involved in the Heydrich case. She had been burned in a house fire. Archie admitted that he was slightly worried that he might be next if it had anything to do with Heydrich.

However, nothing negative relating to these events ever happened to Archie.

Thank goodness the session was recorded!

But these events should give us food for thought. I ask you to remember that I had no idea why Archie wanted a reading and the medium certainly did not know why he wanted a reading. Immediately the session began, the medium spoke about smoke and choking and it transpired that the psychotherapist died in a fire. This did not really give us anything specific by way of evidence but when the medium was taken into a trance state, after initial pleasantries, she launched into information about 'The man of the unholy cross' ... namely a swastika. Not a topic one would easily guess by chance.

Julie had no interest in World War Two, or the German language.

These events would not seem like a case of reincarnation to me, but of a strong influence of overshadowing, almost like a battle between two strengths of consciousness. I would draw the line at possession although, as I said, as time passed the girl did have her hair cut very short and changed her appearance to a more manly style.

It is well known that in many avenues of paranormal activity, when a deceased personality appears to have unfinished business of sorts it can give them the impetus, or motivation, to affect our physical world. In this case the Heydrich persona more or less admitted that he was fearful of moving on, as he did not know what would await him. That would be a powerful motivation to remain.

I leave you to weigh up this account.

Incidentally, the medium later reported that while in trance she could see a lot of people from 'spirit' as clear as day, far clearer than at any time in her life. She said that they were 'lined up' almost like a queue. She was very animated about it and said to me, 'Tricia that was amazing'.

The medium had, and has, no knowledge of anything that was said during the reading and was not given any subsequent information about the death of the psychotherapist.

# 9

# Mediumship

Making sense out of 'seeming' nonsense

## *Materialisation*

It is difficult not to laugh or even scoff at some photos of purported physical mediumship phenomena produced during the latter half of the nineteenth century and early decades of the twentieth. Many of these photos, now found in reference books and on the Internet, appear quite bizarre and absolutely ludicrous. They include doll-like figures that are supposed to be the spirits of deceased individuals; some look like mannequins, others like cardboard cutouts prepared by kindergarten students. Some of the photos show hands only, while others display miniature faces enveloped in a foamy looking substance known as ectoplasm and sometimes called teleplasm, which appears to be flowing from the medium's nose, mouth, solar plexus or ears; even from the nipples or the vagina. Most of the forms are incomplete or rudimentary; some even appear to be flat. A few surviving photos also show fully materialized entities who could pass for comic book characters. We have been told that these full materializations were deceased humans who, in some cases, even embraced living loved ones and carried on conversations with them for a period of time before melting into the floor.

Who in his or her right mind would believe such twaddle to be real? If we rely on some modern references, such as *Wikipedia*, we are assured that it was all fake. We are informed that ectoplasm was nothing more than cheesecloth stuffed in orifices of the body and regurgitated, while confederates in the scam came through trap doors behind curtains and posed as ghosts for gullible people. They claim that wires were rigged around the dark rooms to tilt the tables and make it appear that objects were floating about, while the voices heard around the room came from clever ventriloquists. There was, the debunkers explain, no end to the ingenuity of the many charlatans who took advantage of emotionally, fragile people sometimes mourning the loss of loved ones and oblivious to the deceptive methods of amateur magicians.

What is especially curious and perplexing about all of this supposed humbug is why those alleged mediums thought that anyone would think it real. Did they expect their victims to be so dim-witted, so utterly stupid as to believe all that claptrap was authentic?

You will gather that I am speaking tongue in cheek.

Unfortunately many people believe all of the negative reports.

I have no doubt that there were many incidences of fraud but the fact is, however, that thousands of people, including a good number of distinguished scientists and scholars, did accept some of it as genuine paranormal phenomena.

One such scientist was Charles Richet, a French physiologist, chemist, bacteriologist, pathologist, psychologist, and professor of medicine at the University of Paris. He also distinguished himself by winning the 1913 Nobel Prize in medicine and physiology for his research on anaphylaxis, which is the sensitivity of the body to alien protein substances. He further contributed much to research on the nervous system, anaesthesia, serum therapy, and neuromuscular stimuli and also served as editor of the *Revue Scientifique* for twenty-four years while contributing to many other scientific publications. How could such a man be so shamelessly duped, not just once but on dozens of occasions with different mediums?

The debunkers would have you believe that this brilliant man suddenly lost his mind and critical faculty when researching mediums. This was not the case.

Richet wrote in his 1923 book, *Thirty Years of Psychical Research*:

> This ectoplasmic formation at the expense of the physiological organism of the medium is now beyond all dispute. It is prodigiously strange, prodigiously unusual, and it would seem so unlikely to be credible; but we must give in to the facts. Yes it is absurd; but no matter – it is true.

Richet frequently collaborated with Gustave Geley, a French physician and Laureate of the French Medical Faculty at the University of Lyons, in his investigation of mediums. Geley, who gained some fame from his research in anaesthetics and various diseases including smallpox, stressed that his experiments with mediums were carried out under strict controls in his laboratory, behind locked doors. These experiments included a complete invasive search of the medium beforehand. The searches went so far as to include ruling out hidden objects in the rectum and vagina.

Geley proclaimed in his 1920 book, *From the Unconscious to the Conscious*, "I do not say merely, 'there was no trickery,' I say, 'there was no possibility of trickery".

One of the mediums studied by Richet and Geley was Marthe Béraud, a young French woman referred to for privacy purposes as Eva C. These two scientists along with several associates observed the materialization process with Eva from beginning to end. "It was formed, developed, and disappeared under my own eyes," Geley wrote. "However, unexpected, strange or impossible such a manifestation may appear, I have no right to put forward the slightest doubt as to its reality".

As the two researchers explained it, Eva sat in a cabinet to protect her from disturbing influences and from the action of bright light, although there was sufficient light in the rest of the room for observation purposes. The phenomenon would sometimes appear after a few minutes, but at times it would take more than an hour. Eva, in a light hypnotic state, would sigh and moan from time to time. Geley described it much like a woman in childbirth and explained that, "These moans reach their height just when the manifestation begins; they lessen or cease when the forms are complete".

Richet said that the ectoplasm exuded by Eva, usually from her mouth but at other times from the top of her head, her nipples and the ends of her fingers, was initially invisible. He added, "Then one observes a whitish steam taking the shape of gauze or muslin, in which a hand or arm develops, gains consistency, then moves".

Geley wrote,

> We have seen a hand emerge from a mass of the substance. "We have seen a white mass become a face; we have seen in a few moments the representation of a head give place to that of a hand; we have been able, by the concordant evidence of sight and touch, to perceive the passage of the inorganic amorphous

> substance into a formal organic representation having for the moment all the attributes of life – in flesh and bone, to use a popular expression.

They further observed the materialized matter disappear, melt into the original substance, and be absorbed into the body of the medium. Geley assumed that the amorphous substance was inorganic, but I feel that may not necessarily have been the case.

Although Richet had witnessed a complete materialization with Eva some years earlier in Algiers, all of the materializations he witnessed with Geley were partial or incomplete, some of them even flat. However, the fact that nearly all of the forms and objects produced by Eva were rudimentary, fragmentary, amorphous or defective in one way or another did not suggest fraud to them. Geley in particular was quite clear about this as he declared that they served as evidence of her good faith by asking the question, "How should the medium, ignorant as she was of natural science, have conceived the idea of simulating a rudiment?" To support his position he mentioned that he had seen in certain cases a face appear flat, and then become three dimensional, entirely or partially.

Geley concluded that the materializations were *ideoplastic* – moulded by the thoughts of invisible entities – and the incomplete or aberrant forms were the result of "a force whose metapsychic output is weak and whose means of execution are weaker still". He also thought that in some cases the medium's power was insufficient to produce the desired effect and the materializations stalled before completion, but in other cases the directing entities lacked the ability to effectively project the intended image.

One might infer from Geley's more detailed explanation that while the entities or spirits were attempting to project images into the ectoplasm by thought, their ability to do so varies as much as artistic ability varies among humans. Lending some credence to Geley's conclusions is Richet's experience in one experiment in which a "communicating spirit" said that he could not materialize because he could not remember what he looked like when alive.

> In a later experiment, this same spirit materialized in body but without a face, all this suggesting again that the success of the materialization appears to depend upon the ability of the particular spirit to visualize his or her old self and project that thought-image into the ectoplasm.

While Geley came to accept that spirits of the dead were behind it all, Richet remained sceptical and "scientific," preferring to believe that some unknown aspect of the medium's subconscious was responsible for the phenomenon of materialization. He expressed his frustration stating:

> To ask a physician, a physicist, or a chemist to admit that a form that has a circulation of blood, warmth, and muscles, that exhales carbonic acid, has weight, speaks, and thinks, can issue from a human body is to ask of him an intellectual effort that is really painful.

This is a good example of cognitive dissonance.

His thinking was divided as he had recently examined the materialized Bien Boa, checking its, or his, heart rate, respirations, etc., finding them to be different from that of the medium in a normal state. However, Richet was later quoted as saying that the spirit hypothesis "Explains the facts more easily" than does the subconscious explanation. Good point. As far as a physical manifestation is concerned this would especially be true if the medium had no previous knowledge of the materialized figure.

Baron Albert von Schrenck-Notzing, a German neurologist, was just as certain as Richet and Geley that fraud was not a factor with Eva C. Over a four-year period (1909-1913), he carried out 180 experiments with her, also requiring an examination of all cavities of the body, including the private parts, to rule out anything being smuggled into the laboratory room.

It must have been hard work being a medium in those days! They certainly must have dedicated themselves to the work.

Schrenck-Notzing was a serious researcher who also studied a number of other mediums over a 40-year period. He declared, "The productions of Eva C. are undoubtedly genuine, and only a malicious prejudice could doubt the reality of the occurrences". He further observed that the artistic performances in the productions "Are of various levels, from the highest artistic power down to an amateur awkwardness". He noted that materializations usually liquefied or evaporated when exposed to too much light or touch. "The mysterious intelligence, which appears to be concerned in this preparatory work evidently wishes to make face and head types optically visible, but requires a certain time for doing so, which may amount to as much as an hour". He wrote this in his 1923 book, *Phenomena of Materialization*, further noting that the materialized hands sometimes showed no signs of life and at other times showed their living character by grasping objects held out to them; even by digging their nails into the skin of his hands.

Richet, Geley, and Schrenck-Notzing also studied Eusapia Palladino, another physical medium who was written off as a charlatan by more casual observers of her time, and in some modern references. Richet stated, "Even if there were no other medium than Eusapia in the world, her manifestations would suffice to establish scientifically the reality of telekinesis and ectoplasmic forms".

T. Glen Hamilton, a Canadian physician who undertook an investigation of mediums producing much the same phenomena as Eva C., stated, "To suggest that these trained observers were all deceived by fraudulent operations, those stupid and very tiresome performances which mislead no one but the uninformed and gullible, is to offer an explanation which offends our reason and shows wilful indifference to truth".

Over a period of some five years (1928-1934), Hamilton, working with a number of associates, observed hundreds of materializations and photographed many of them. He stated,

> I regard teleplasm (ectoplasm) as a highly sensitive substance, responsive to other-world energies and at the same time visible to us in the physical world". Hamilton concluded, "It therefore constitutes an intervening substance by means of which transcendental intelligences are enabled by ideoplastic or other unknown processes to transmit their conception of certain energy forms which appear objective to them, into the terms of our world and understanding.

This is similar to Geley's interpretation.

The ideoplastic process was alluded to again at a small gathering in England during 1912, when William T. Stead, a victim of the (already mentioned) *Titanic* disaster earlier that year, materialized in front of a group gathered with American medium Etta Wriedt. According to one person in the group, William Usborne Moore, a retired admiral of the British navy turned psychical researcher, the materialized Stead said that there were souls on his side who had the power of sensing people (mediums) who could be used for communication. One such soul helped him to find mediums and showed him how to make his presence known. It was explained to him that he had to visualize himself among the people in the flesh and imagine that he was standing there in the flesh with a strong light thrown upon himself. He had to "Hold the visualization very deliberately and in detail, and keep it fixed upon my mind, that at that moment I *was* there and they were conscious of it," adding that the people at one sitting were able to see only his face because he had seen himself as only a face. "I imagined the part they would recognize me by". It was in the same way, he said, that he was able to speak to them. He stood by the most sensitive person there, apparently the medium, concentrated his mind on a short sentence, and repeated it with much emphasis and deliberation until the medium could hear at least part of it.

In effect all, or at least some, of those bizarre manifestations surviving in photographs may very well have been genuine spirit productions. As already stated they may have been imperfect either because the medium lacked power or because the spirit entities attempting to show themselves lacked the ability or know-how to project their images into the ectoplasm. It might be likened to asking the average person today to draw a portrait of him- or herself. Only a few would succeed with a recognizable likeness. Many would resemble cartoon characters or stick figures. Also it should be kept in mind that people from earlier years, before the development of photography, may not have had a fixed idea of what they looked like. How many people today would remember what they looked like at a much younger age if they did not have photographs to remind them?

Geley stated the following, "In the science and philosophy of ectoplasmic formation resides the great secret and the great mystery, a revelation of the highest knowledge, a divine consummation hitherto denied to mortals". He probably assumed that science would have a better grasp on it a hundred years later. How wrong he was.

Things have not really moved on at all.

Even during the 1850s, long before the experiments by Richet, Geley, Shrenck-Notzing and Hamilton, others gave credibility to this strange physical phenomenon. Robert Hare, a professor of chemistry at the University of Pennsylvania and a renowned inventor, investigated a number of mediums with the intent of debunking them. However, he came to the conclusion that mediumship was real, even if there were a number of frauds mixed in with the real ones (as in any walk of life).

Hare asked a communicating spirit what it was all about and why there was so much crazy stuff. He was informed that the various phenomena were, "A deliberate effort on the part of the inhabitants of the higher spheres to break through the partition which has interfered with the attainment, by mortals, of a correct idea of their destiny after death". To carry out this intention, he was told, a delegation of advanced spirits had been appointed. He was further informed that lower spirits were allowed to take part in the undertaking because they were better able to make mechanical movements and loud rappings than those on the higher realms. It became clear to Hare and other researchers that in their opinion the spirits were experimenting on their side just as we were on ours.

After declaring his belief in spirits, Hare came under attack by his scientific colleagues, a well-known reaction that still occurs today. However, he remained steadfast in his new worldview by stating, "It is a well-known saying," as he lamented the conflicting views of his critics, "that there is but one step between the sublime and ridiculous'.

In conclusion, it behoves us to remember that all of the investigators mentioned here were nobody's fool; they were highly intelligent, well educated, honest and scrupulous in their work, whose only motive was to seek out the truth about the phenomenon.

Extracts from *JSPR*. Vol. 77: 89-101. April, 2013.
Evans, H. (2002). *Seeing Ghosts: Experiences of the paranormal*. London. John Murray.

## *Jesse Shepard*

There are many recognised forms of mediumship. With mental mediumship some mediums purport to see an image of a deceased person in their mind's eye through a process described as clairvoyance; some hear the voice by means of clairaudience and some simply sense or feel what is being conveyed to them by means of clairsentience. (Just 'feeling' or 'knowing' the information.)

Within physical mediumship there have been many well-attested direct voice mediums including Leslie Flint and John Sloan, where, in this process, the voice of a deceased person appears to come through the medium or from the nearby surroundings. As already mentioned there have also been some wonderful materialisation mediums, where an actual figure is produced, such as Eva C, Queenie Nixon and Gordon Higginson. As if this was not strange enough, there are some other forms of mediumship, which surpass all expectations and seeming credulity.

To illustrate this 'loose' category I would like to highlight the talents of the pianist Jesse Shepard, born Jesse Francis Grierson Shepard, who was sometimes referred to as the musical medium. The question is, was he a genius, a medium or a bit of both?

I will provide you with a little background about this most unusual gentleman to help put the following, seemingly bizarre, series of events in perspective.

He was born in England in 1848 and taken to the United States of America as an infant by his parents. His talent for psychometry and clairvoyance began to appear when he was around nineteen years old. In case anyone does not know, psychometry is the talent of gaining relevant paranormal information from an object: either about the object itself, the person who brought it or information relating to a deceased person with a connection to that object. This seems to be done by the medium in some unknown way 'sensing' the object, or on occasion, the contents of a sealed envelope.

At this point in his life, Jesse was taking piano lessons but he was an average musician and his younger sister was a better piano player than he was. However, by the age of twenty-one something extraordinary had happened; his talent almost inexplicably blossomed beyond anyone's wildest dreams. He then, with no knowledge of the language and hardly a penny in his pocket, set out for Paris where he received almost immediate acclaim as a 'Piano improvisator par excellence'.

He soon became a welcome guest at fashionable Parisian salons where he played for the higher echelons of society and arts; and indeed those with distinguished titles. In addition to his flair for the piano he was blessed with a beautiful and extraordinary voice. He sang in many prestigious locations including the Basilica of Montmartre and the Cathedral of Notre Dame. In fact he was the 'darling' of the time in Paris; no doubt gaining rewards from his wealthy social circle of friends. Novelist and playwright Alexandre Dumas the elder told Shepard, 'With your gifts you will find all doors open before you'.

When the Franco-Prussian War broke out, Jesse returned to London where he continued giving recitals for the distinguished and social elite. However in 1870 he also advertised in a London paper that his psychic services were available.

He listed his talents as, 'Clairvoyant, prophetic, psychometric sittings, diagnosis of disease, and discovery of mediumistic faculties' with the addendum that, 'Musical manifestations are not given at the same sitting'.

It appears that his psychic talents first appeared in 1867 but we do not seem to have any more information as to the progression of their development.

The musical manifestations seemed to have developed around that same time. These manifestations could include the sound of other invisible instruments being heard accompanying Shepard on the piano, and on occasion also other voices. Many very sensible people testified to that.

He could also seemingly play the piano magnificently under the 'control' or 'influence' of Mozart, Beethoven, Liszt, Berlioz, Chopin and many others. As far as I can ascertain, the quality and authenticity of the music was accepted by those who know about these things.

After eight months in London he moved on to St Petersburg where his circle of friends included the King and Queen of Prussia. Again, he did this with no knowledge of Russian, and only enough money to last him a week.

In St Petersburg he was again accommodated by Russia's wealthy elite.

In 1874, when he was twenty-six years old, he returned to the United States of America where in New York he spent ten days with Madame Blavatsky and Colonel Olcott, the co-founders of Theosophy. Olcott stated in his book *Old Diary Leaves* that 'Shepard not only gave mediumistic performances but entered into the spirit of things by going into trance and singing Russian songs'. Unfortunately Shepard and Blavatsky had a personality conflict and she later accused Jessie of having a music master teach him the Russian songs; perhaps out of jealousy; who knows?

He then spent the best part of twelve years roaming the world, making a fortune by his wits and talents.

In Chicago he held a series of séances in the home of another medium and, according to the daughter of the respected Hudson Tuttle, 'Strange and unaccountable phenomena' nightly occurred. She testified to the medium's most amazing performance where he sang simultaneously in two voices, base and soprano, his control singing in one voice and an Egyptian spirit the other. Accompanying him was 'another spirit' playing the harp.

Throughout his career this dual toned singing left his listeners in a state of bewildered shock.

She also stated that between musical pieces he would 'under spirit influence' give mediumistic information to the sitters describing their spirit friends.

Around 1887 he returned to San Diego where he was able to reside in surroundings of complete opulence.

Private séances were held in the music room. It is reported that his music was so unearthly it was 'simply indescribable'. Again, guests claimed that they could hear choirs of voices led by Shepard's own singing, now soaring to the heights of soprano then dropping to a deep bass. Others on occasion heard invisible drums, tambourines and trumpets, sometimes with voices coming from the open end of the trumpets.

During his years spent in Europe, Shepard wrote essays on art, philosophy and his own paranormal experiences. In 1899 he published a book entitled *Modern Mysticism* under his two middle names Francis Grierson. In 1921 he then published another book at his own expense, entitled *Psycho-Phone Messages.* He was indeed a man of many talents.

Jesse Sheppard was now not only the 'darling' of Paris but also the 'darling' of Kings. One of his performances was held at the Imperial Palace of Gatchina for the Tsar of Russia. Another before a reunion of three royal houses at Cumberland Palace in Gmunden, Austria, where his hostess was the Duchess of Cumberland, sister of the Empress of Russia. Other guests included the Queen of Greece, Queen of Hanover, Queen of Denmark and H.R.H. Reigning Duke of Saxe-Altenburg.

After the performance everyone present complimented him on the beauty of his music and the Queen of Denmark remarked that Shepard's piano playing had the effect of four hands playing instead of two.

Throughout the years there were multifarious testimonies about his wonderful music, but he did not always utilise his 'paranormal' abilities in a performance. He carefully chose his audiences to exhibit these talents, performing only to audiences who would appreciate them.

Mr Henry Kiddle, superintendent of schools in New York, had Shepard living with him in his own house for twelve months, during which time Shepard performed for him on many occasions. He testified to the fact that during one of these performances he heard him play under the control of Mozart, executing a magnificent impromptu symphony while delivering a learned philosophical dissertation under the influence of Aristotle at the same time.

I know that all of this sounds extremely bizarre but are we to assume that all of the witnesses to Shepard's performances were under the influence of some mass hypnosis similar to that of the fairy tale 'The King's New Clothes?'

Due to the credibility of the witnesses and the number of years that he had been performing, plus the enormous amount of testimony by witnesses, I would find that an unlikely scenario.

Just when you thought things could not get any more unbelievable your boggle factor limit will really kick in with this next account.

The location was the Royal Residence of Prince Adam Wisniewski in Rome. The year 1894. Members of the Italian court, social personages, patrons and performers of the arts had gathered here to witness a musical séance by Shepard. He was suited and booted in flamboyant style with frilly lace cuffs, etc. I have a mental image of Liberace!

The guests were placed in a circle around the piano and the room was darkened. As he struck the first chord, tiny lights flickered in every corner of the room. Some great composers from past centuries ostensibly then arrived to perform their latest compositions through the nimble fingers of the medium.

A globe of light and three raps on the Prince's knee then announced the arrival of Chopin and French novelist George Sand respectively. The music was completely in accordance with Chopin's style. Jesse finished with a pianissimo fraught with despair, 'A prayer to God for Poland'. It is reported that this sombre mood was dispelled by the arrival of Mozart whose unique and melodious music danced to an airy climax.

The Prince reported that the most marvellous incident of the evening was the arrival of Berlioz. It was the first time that Berlioz had played through Shepard and on arrival he expressed the opinion that the piano was tuned too low for his music. (Remember that Shepard was also clairvoyant and clairaudient.) Berlioz then tuned it a tone higher. The Prince continued,

> For ten minutes we heard the spirits working with the piano, with the lid closed. When the recital continued, at the first sound we observed that the instrument was about two notes higher. Then Berlioz played sweet, ideal music. It seemed as if we heard the little bells of a country churchyard. When this piece finished, Berlioz, with the aid of several other spirits, restored the instrument to its first tuning and began playing on its ordinary tone while the lid was still shut. Several spirits came afterwards, each speaking their own language.

Shepard himself still only spoke English and a little French, but when he was in trance it appears that the 'spirits' spoke through him in many languages including German, Hebrew, Russian and Arabic.

After that séance the Prince reported that, 'Mr Shepard was much exhausted and had to retire to rest'.

The late, and highly respected, Nandor Fodor wrote in his book *Between Two Worlds*, 'No musical party by the Mad Hatter could sound more preposterous than this account. It leaves breathless the most ardent spiritualists'.

Fodor made arguments for and against these strange phenomena, but ended up as confused as the rest of us, in a state of cognitive dissonance where the facts contradict any ideas of what he thought was possible.

By 1927 Shepard was trying to shake off his 'psychic abilities' and be recognised for his written works as Francis Grierson. Despite his efforts, fellow authors and publishers failed to express enough interest in his work. Eventually all sources of income failed and he became destitute. Because of this, Zona Gale, a Pulitzer Prize winning novelist, wrote to friends in Los Angeles and persuaded them to arrange a benefit dinner to assist and honour Shepard. In the meantime he had pawned the last of his possessions, a gold watch given to him by King Edward VII.

On May 29, 1927, following the dinner Shepard entertained the guests with 'Marvellous instantaneous compositions on the piano'. After some time he announced that his last piece would be his Grand Egyptian March. It was a haunting and mystical rendition with mighty chords alternating with soft chords creating mental images of Gods, Temples and Empires of the past. It appeared to be entirely exhausting for him.

When he finished he sat perfectly still as he often did, with his head bent forward and his fingers on the keys. There was enthusiastic applause but no response. Many seconds passed. A Mr Tonner felt an anxious grip in his stomach. He arose and walked over to the piano to find that Shepard was dead.

It was true: at the age of seventy-nine he died as dramatically as he had lived his life.

I leave you to absorb this account, weighing up the pros and cons. It is a lot to digest. But thoughtfully consider the reported quality of the music and phenomena plus the enormous number of witnesses, their credibility and the consistency of the accounts over a very large number of years.

This summary of the life and death of Jesse Shepard is merely a taste of the wealth of testimonies to his abilities in a flamboyant, rich and very colourful life.

## *Ros Cattanagh*

Ros Cattanagh was a merchant banker who lived in London. She was well educated, erudite and not one to suffer fools gladly.

Her son, David, died when he was nineteen years old. At that time Leslie Flint, the direct voice medium, was in his heyday and Ros found her way to his sessions. After a relatively short time she became convinced by the evidence that the voice coming through for her in the sessions was indeed her son. This conclusion was arrived at from both the sound of his voice and the content of the communication. She then became actively interested in seeking evidence for survival and, many years later, held the position of President of the London Spiritual Mission in Pembridge Place, London. It was then that I became acquainted with her.

I had been invited to give a short talk at her church about psychical research and evidence for survival and my talk was to be followed by medium Gordon Smith who would give a demonstration of mediumship. Ros did not really know me at that time and had never heard me speak. In true form, before I took the podium, she pointedly told me not to speak for too long as people had come to hear the medium. I liked her approach and found it humorous, and, as instructed, I kept my talk evidential, informative and to the point.

When Ros then arose to introduce the medium, she looked sideways at me and announced to the audience that she had never known twenty minutes to pass so quickly! That was it; I was 'in'.

Subsequently, I was invited back to the church a few times and it was during one of these visits that the following occurred.

But before I launch into my tale I have to mention that the medium Albert Best was also a regular guest at the church and very popular. Albert, a very humble man, was well known for the quality of his mediumship and for many years he received invitations to demonstrate in many different countries, one of his favourites being India. He was very proud of this. From every aspect he and Ros were polar opposites but they had struck up a really respectful friendship with each other through the years. I am not saying that they never had words, but it was always in a good spirit.

At one of my talks there Archie Roy was present. After the talk the three of us had an evening meal and a good chat, and he retired to his room for the night leaving Ros and me sitting alone in the lounge of this beautiful building. After some conversation and possibly a small sherry she told me the following:

She claimed that she could always tell when Albert was 'getting something' from spirit by the expression on his face. On one particular evening she and Albert had been sitting on individual chairs in the lounge that I mentioned earlier and she said to him, 'You have that silly look on your face again; what is it?' Albert raised a finger and slowly pointed to a cabinet in the lounge and said, 'There is something in there that relates to David'.

'Nonsense', she replied haughtily. 'I know everything that is in that cabinet' Albert said, 'No you are wrong – there is a piece of paper in there with his writing on it and it is written in pencil'.

To prove her point, somewhat reluctantly she emptied out the section that Albert had alluded to. She pulled everything apart and could find nothing relating to Albert's statement. Feeling triumphant she told him again that he was wrong. He insisted that she had missed something and made her look again. This time as she looked more carefully in one particular folder (where she had already looked) and leafed through every page where she found a piece of paper jammed between two sheets. She was shocked to find text there written in pencil, and it was David's handwriting. She showed me the paper.

She also told me that on another occasion, they were sitting again on individual chairs in the same lounge, reading newspapers. The chair that Ros was sitting on was a Parker-Knoll type with a cushion set on a wooden base and below the wood was a spring arrangement. I was actually sitting on this chair when she told me the following. Albert said to her, 'Stand up!' Not terribly amused she stood up. He then said, 'Lift the cushion'. She did so, looked at the seat and saw only the wooden base on top of the springs. He said, 'Sit down'. Somewhat grudgingly she did so, replaced the cushion and sat down. A few minutes later he said, 'Stand up! Reluctantly she did so. Again, he said, 'Lift the cushion'. This time she was astounded to see a largish photograph of David looking up at her from the wooden base. No one had moved between the two events.

Albert, who was not terribly demonstrative, just nodded his head and returned to reading a newspaper. Such was their friendship.

She was a wonderful lady and I feel privileged to have known her.

As a point of information, when I visited Albert in his home I, along with any other visitor, was shown all of the presents and artefacts that he has received from Indian royalty. He was not boastful, just proud.

## *Belmez*

A gentle, traditional Spanish lady named Maria had lived happily in a particular house at Calle Real 5 in Belmez, Spain for many years. In 1971, something changed. She began to notice marks appearing on the concrete floor in her kitchen. These markings could not be cleaned; she tried everything to remove them, to no avail. As time passed it appeared as though these marks were forming into shapes of faces and other body parts. Maria was a devout catholic and very concerned as she thought that some evil force had infested her house. A local priest assisted her by dowsing the house and in a particular area of the kitchen his dowsing pendulum became very active over one section of the floor.

Maria decided to have the floor lifted at that spot and deep down in the earth foundations the remains of a human skeleton were found. Maria then had the whole floor dug up and replaced with a new concrete floor.

Hoping that a ceremony would put an end to the marks appearing on the floor, the remains were given a Christian burial.

Maria's relief was short lived when, sometime later, new images began to appear on the new floor. The images seemed to form at different rates – some took minutes while others took hours. Maria observed that it was as if a mist appeared on top of the concrete and when it disappeared another image was there.

People around the world heard about the phenomenon and Maria was besieged for years by reporters and the media. Incidentally, as far as I'm aware, she did not profit financially from the attention apart from being given a television by a German television company.

As these events became so well known, the street name was changed to La Calle de las Caras (The street of faces). However, by 1990 Maria had become despondent with it all, and was still trying to get an explanation for the phenomenon. She contacted the Spanish Society for Psychical Research.

At this point in time many people had come to view the floor markings and had offered various explanations for their appearance. One theory was that the marks were made by footprints – size 39. This seemed most unlikely given that some of the images looked like heads with hair, faces or torsos with arms and legs.

Another explanation was that they were caused in some way by artistic materials within the concrete and another, possibly the best, was that Maria got up every night and drew on the concrete herself.

This might appeal to those of a cynical nature except that the 'drawings' were not actually on the top of the concrete but appeared to be just under the surface.

When the Spanish SPR investigated they took scrapings of the concrete and had the concrete analysed in a scientific laboratory, which showed that the composition included elements of Zinc, Barium, Copper, Chromium, Lead and Phosphorus. I am advised that this is a perfectly normal mix, which showed no evidence of drawing materials.

They also made a video of the floor and surroundings, where one can see clearly the 'faces' and other markings.

In 1991, respected Spanish researcher Manual Cabello visited the house and he also took a video of the floor. When the 1990 video was compared with that of 1991 it was obvious that the faces and body images had actually moved to a different part of the floor. An image of a head, which was close to a skirting board in the 1990 video, was inches away from the skirting board in 1991. The images appeared to be dynamic as though drifting just under the surface of the concrete. As time went by more drawings appeared in the hallway.

Later it was discovered that the house had been built on the site of an old necropolis. Whether that was a factor or not, who can say?

Maria passed away around 2001. Whether the faces are still there I know not. Some people say that Maria was possibly unwittingly acting as some kind of medium. But if that was the case why did she live there for decades when nothing happened?

One thing that we do know is that it was truly mysterious and has never been satisfactorily explained. I noted from the videos that some of the faces did appear to be quite 'disturbed'.

## *The Gold Leaf Lady*

In examining this case Professor Stephen Braude, a well respected and world-renowned philosopher, departed from his normal topics of investigation. His book, *Immortal Remains*, is a classic in the realms of psychical research, and was written and posited from a philosopher's point of view. The subsequent Gold Leaf Lady case resulted in another excellent book by Braude, *The Gold Leaf Lady and Other Parapsychological Investigations.*

This book is written from his personal viewpoint; understandably so as much of it considers his personal investigations and the "usual" gripes that ensue from people who have done no work whatsoever in that particular topic but are eager to point out where flaws may have occurred within investigations. Note that sceptics always put emphasis on the word *may.* Because the phenomena produced from cases, such as that the gold leaf lady, can actually be seen, the debunker clings to the *a priorism* that it must be fraud, delusion or use of a sloppy research protocol. Why should a researcher of Braude's calibre suddenly become sloppy when his life's work has been fastidious to the nth degree? Perhaps a gullibility gene has just come into play? I think not.

He didn't set out to make any friends in reporting his findings within this investigation. He stated that:

> The history of science is more than a series of discoveries, failures, tests of hypotheses, and so on. To some extent it's also a tale of people behaving very strangely – and on occasion, very badly. Historians and sociologists have shown that scientists often fail to be the models of objectivity, virtue and clear thinking we'd like them to be. Like everyone else, they have confusions, hidden agendas, fears and other frailties that sometimes lead to less than admirable – or at least curious – behaviour.

The subject, Katie, was a Florida woman who could, on occasion, produce the appearance of a foil like substance, which looked like "gold leaf" on her skin. This could appear on any part of her body. At first it appeared as if it was coming through her skin, but this did not seem to be the case as, eventually, items within her vicinity could also have "gold leaf" deposited on them. In fact it is not actually gold leaf per se, and his book goes into detail about it. Braude had studied this woman for many years and brings his own rigour and insight to the investigation. He also describes in detail some of Katie's other abilities, which encompass a wide variety of phenomena.

Katie was born into a poor family in Tennessee. Her education was minimal; she could write her name but couldn't form words and could barely do simple arithmetic. Braude was impressed by her apparent honesty and willingness to be studied for no financial reward. She appeared to be a very kind and sensitive soul.

It was noted that sometimes months would pass without any foil appearing on her skin and then it would manifest for weeks at a time.

When the phenomenon originally occurred, Katie's skin would glisten and then form droplets of, what seemed to be moisture, which then changed to the appearance of layers of foil. This made observers think that it was coming through her skin but that did not account for the foil, which subsequently appeared on her clothes and other objects in her vicinity.

The amounts of foil produced were often profuse. Braude sent samples to a laboratory for analysis which showed that its composition was approximately 80% copper and 20% zinc and also contained minimal amounts of sodium, magnesium, potassium, silver, cadmium, manganese, arsenic and lead. This meant that if Katie was producing it from her own body she would have had to have stored lethal amounts of metal in her system, which would not have been possible.

The interesting thing to me is that in the analysis there was no sign of gold or anything that resembled it. We also have to consider the question of its texture.

The laboratory that examined the leaf concluded that the composition of the foil was similar to a commercial foil called 'brass leaf' or 'Dutch metal'. They also determined that Katie's foil had the same granular structure as ordinary pressed or rolled leaf.

It came to light that it was around 1986 when Katie first 'produced' this foil – not long after her second marriage to 'Tom'. By all accounts this was a difficult and psychologically abusive relationship. Tom appears to have been obsessed with money and would say things to her along the lines of, 'Can you not do something useful to make money?'

So, did her subconscious in some way act on that challenge which resulted in the production of this 'gold'?

How this might be possible I could not even guess but perhaps similar in some way to external phenomena produced in personalised poltergeist cases or stigmata.

In 1990 Braude put Katie under the experimental 'microscope'. He was instrumental in acquiring the assistance of Dean Radin – a well-known and respected parapsychologist – along with a magician, Chris Chacon. Chacon was a skilled conjurer. Chris was provided with a sample of Katie's foil and Dutch leaf. After examination he determined that it would really be extremely difficult to manipulate this clingy material. It became clear to him that Katie could not inconspicuously place this material on herself or the surroundings while under strict experimental conditions.

Stephen Braude has been in very close proximity to Katie on various occasions where he has observed for himself this glistening of her skin, the formation of a droplet, even in the corner of her eye, and has watched that droplet turn to foil. He is a fastidious researcher and would not easily be duped.

To date, as far as I know, more research needs to be carried out on this subject. As you can imagine, her husband is not best pleased.

I am merely drawing your attention to the fact that such a case as this exists. I would think that the phenomenon produced has nothing whatsoever to do with survival of personality after death but an example of just how amazing we are as human beings and how our subconscious responds under stress.

For a detailed description of the intricacies of this case I recommend that *The Gold Leaf Lady* should be on your reading list. Braude's book contains photographs of Katie and the gold leaf.

Braude's book on this subject is a "must read" for anyone interested in the pursuit of psychical research and the difficulties that are presented in doing so. However, he is optimistic about such research and is excited by possibilities in the knowledge that there is so much in the world for which we do not as yet have a suitable scientific model.

He waxes lyrically about the dedicated debunker's approach to cases such as these, and sleazy scepticism whereby they publically announce that the particular case is a fraud, without even trying to amass all of the studies and relevant information.

His excitement is contagious and I can heartily recommend this provocative, and at times perhaps controversial, book to you.

## *Uri Geller*

You probably think of Uri as a charismatic entertainer and are asking yourself, 'Why is he being mentioned in this book?'

I will tell you. He is much more than an entertainer and has demonstrated beyond doubt that he has abilities not given to many, and I don't mean just the well-known spoon bending.

There has never been any doubt that Uri was and is an accomplished dowser; in fact that is where he made most of his money. For years he was employed by companies to dowse for water, mineral, oil – in fact anything that was required. He also claims to have been a remote viewer for various government agencies and I am sure that is correct.

As Uri is such a showman, almost a Liberace of the paranormal, it can sometimes be difficult to take him seriously. However, many people have observed his metal bending abilities, including myself, Professor

Archie Roy, and other psychical researchers such as Maurice Grosse and Guy Lyon Playfair.

Some years ago, Archie was on the same television programme as Uri. Off camera and during leisure time, Uri was demonstrating spoon bending. As Archie watched the spoon bending, he ran forward and grabbed it out of Uri's hand. The spoon had been lifted in plain sight out of a bowl of cutlery supplied by the caterers. As Archie held it he was surprised to see that it continued to bend. This was when Archie realised that the bowls of the spoons do not bend downwards, but the bowls of the spoons bend up towards the person holding the spoon. Therefore, critics who say that Uri rubs the neck of the spoon to weaken the metal so that the bowl falls off, are clearly wrong.

More recently I saw him at a book signing in Glasgow. A friend and I arrived there early so that we could get a good view of anything that might happen. We sat in the second row, just slightly to one side. The book being promoted was actually about Uri and was written by a very sceptical journalist who set out to investigate him. The author spoke for a time and then Uri took to the (very small) stage. We were about four feet away from him. We had watched people arriving, many of whom had a spoon in their hands. After a time he asked for a spoon and a small boy ran forward and thrust a spoon into his hand. After no time at all, Uri lightly touched it and, yes, the bowl started slowly to bend upwards. The triumphant child took it home later. The audience offered a few other spoons; they also bent in the same manner. I did speak to Uri afterwards and he was indeed very charming.

Maurice Grosse became quite friendly with Uri and, by mutual agreement, subjected him to all kinds of experimentation. Under test conditions, Maurice claimed that he witnessed Uri bend a thick piece of steel by a few degrees simply by concentrating on it. I was also shown a four-inch screw bolt about a half-inch thick that he bent under test conditions. Maurice was a successful professional inventor and he would not easily be duped. Guy Lyon Playfair was also a positive witness to Uri's abilities and co-authored a book with him titled *The Geller Effect.*

It was some time after Uri became known for his psychokinesis abilities when he met psychical researcher Dr Andrija Puharich, a physicist and medical doctor.

At his first public meeting observing Uri, Puharich, initially very sceptical, was invited to hold a broken watch in his hand. He shook it – it worked for a few seconds and then stopped.

Uri refused to touch it, but told Puharich to put it in the palm of a woman's hand. She closed her hand – Uri put his left palm over her hand. After thirty seconds the watch began working and did so for thirty minutes.

Meanwhile, at 2:00 p.m., Uri asked Puharich to take off his watch, a very expensive chronometer, and hold it in his hand. Uri held his hand over Puharich's for ten seconds and asked for the time to be checked. It read 2:32 p.m. The watch had advanced thirty-two minutes. The similarity was noted between this and the woman's watch, which had worked for thirty minutes. This may or may not have been meaningful. Puharich was impressed and concluded that this feat of psychokinesis was unparalleled in his experience. All of this was filmed.

Uri then said that by concentrating his mind he could crack the wedding ring of a woman called Sarah, with the promise that it would not actually be broken. There was no outer evidence of the ring being cracked or broken but it was subsequently sent for analysis to Dr Anton West, a metallurgist in Stanford University, California. Electron microscopy showed that there was indeed a fracture and that fracture was found to be of an unknown type.

It was then agreed that Uri would give Puharich three to four hours of his time each day for experimentation purposes.

In one of the experiments, Uri was asked to concentrate on a pair of bi-metallic strip thermometers. The irons that you use for pressing shirts certainly used to work with bi-metallic strips; they control the temperature of the iron as one strip heats up quicker than the other and that breaks the power contact.

Under perfectly controlled conditions, Uri, even from across the room, was repeatedly able to raise the temperature of a thermometer by mind power alone. He achieved a six to eight degree change on whichever of the instruments was selected.

He was able repeatedly to move a compass needle through ninety degrees, while he was in another room. Pucharich noted that the compass moving experiments seemed to exhaust him. It was also noticed that this seemed to work better if Uri put rubber bands tightly around his left wrist as a tourniquet to block the flow of blood. Why this should be I have no idea.

Uri also displayed the ability to bend a thin stream of water from the tap with his hand held a few centimetres away. This can be done by anyone with an electrically charged piece of plastic: usually a comb, which has just been run though hair, but generally not by a hand.

In science the word *energy* is described as something that has the 'ability to do work'. We can therefore deduce that Uri must be producing some kind of energy that affected the bimetallic metal strips, strips of metal, broken watches, compass needles and a stream of water from the tap. We need not try to define this at the moment – but some kind of energy *must* have been produced to have these effects.

Puharich then devised another test to see if Uri could narrowly direct and control a beam of 'this' energy or whether he produced a scattergun effect by blasting everything in front of him.

He laid out five matchsticks in a row on a glass plate. Using concentration alone Uri was able to move *any selected* matchstick from the five by up to 32 millimetres. That is quite an impressive distance. This was also a repeatable experiment, which showed that Uri *could* precisely direct and control the energy that he was sending / producing, call it what you will.

In another experiment Puharich, in front of several witnesses, took a brass refill cartridge with the number 347299 engraved on it and put it inside a ball point pen and then put the pen into a wooden box. Uri held his hands over the box for a time and another person then opened the box. The pen itself had remained but when they opened it up the cartridge inside had disappeared.

In case you think that Puharich and other witnesses had been fooled, think again. Uri never touched the box at any time and he had no forewarning of the nature of that experiment.

Then things became even more bizarre. A few days later Uri, Puharich and a woman called Iris were in a suburb of Tel Aviv and above a building site they all saw a bluish pulsating light. Uri felt drawn to it and told the others to stay in the car. As he approached he saw a massive object and sensed that he was being drawn into its interior. He believed that he could make out the shape of control panels inside the object. Then a dark shape approached him and put something in his hand. Seconds later he was running back to Puharich. He was holding a brass ballpoint ink refill cartridge with the number 347299 engraved on it.

Puharich and his colleagues had mixed feelings about the whole experimentation set up as they thought that Uri was an "unabashed egomaniac", but, as Puharich said, "I feel that he is so extraordinary that he is worth almost any effort".

Personalities aside, the facts speak for themselves – some people do have unexplained extraordinary talents.

The investigative journalist Jonathan Margolis studied Uri for many years from a very sceptical standpoint; in fact he told me that initially he set out to debunk him. However, after several years, he had to conclude that his claims, borne out by evidence, are absolutely genuine. His findings are laid out in two books: *Uri Geller, Magician or Mystic* and *The Secret Life of Uri Geller: CIA Masterspy?*

Professor J. B. Hasted, atomic physicist and professor of experimental physics at Birkbeck College, University of London stated in an interview in 1997, 'If people say that Uri Geller is a magician, they have simply failed to read the published scientific evidence'.

When cases such as The Gold Leaf Lady, Belmez, Uri Geller and Jesse Shepard come to light, some people prejudge them and roll back their eyes with a ready sneer of disbelief without even studying the evidence. Why do people do this?

In 1882 when the Society for Psychical Research was set up, the members hoped that within a hundred years or so there would be light shed on evidence, which provided an acceptance for, at least some psychic phenomena. Well here we are in 2020 and we are not much further on with this quest. Here are some possible reasons for rejection of evidence:

Religious Fundamentalism: whereby the followers of any particular religious doctrine accept their particular dogma as the be all and end all, and anything outside that cannot be true.

Scientific Fundamentalism: Very similar to the above as they accept the known science of the time to be absolutely correct.

Media Bias & Ignorance: Journalists and programme producers have to follow the policy of whoever pays their salary. They also like to expose would-be shams and fraudulent schemes, which naturally lends itself to sensationalism and makes for good copy. Aligning with this is the way that mediums are portrayed. [Author's note: I remember seeing a television programme in which they used mediums with a good track record in bringing information from those departed and the task that they were given was to identify which cars in a car park contained a person hiding in the boot! That is like asking a person proficient in the cultivation of pears to give a talk about growing broccoli.]

Fear: Scientists and others in highly educated positions may fear for their reputations if they are seen to be interested in researching the paranormal.

Being influenced by people allegedly providing inference of fraud: Many sceptics come forward to explain how certain phenomena "could have" or "might have" been accomplished by clever sleight of hand or other deception. They rarely, if ever, complete a task in the same conditions as that of a genuine person with a paranormal ability. It is they who are indeed operating 'sleight of mind'.

I reiterate that it behoves us all to examine the actual evidence in all cases.

# 10

# Home Circles

Before the arrival of radio, television and mobile phones many people (in this part of the world) spent their leisure time holding regular séances in their homes. We know, historically, they were popular in Victorian times and the appetite continued and still does to a certain extent today.

About twelve years ago someone whom I would trust completely gave this next account to me. In later life he became a minister of religion. I will call him James Y. In the 1950s he had been invited to participate in a home circle séance in his local area.

The regular sitters held bi-weekly meetings in a 'prefab' in Knightswood, Glasgow. Prefabricated houses were produced after the Second World War for use as affordable, reasonably comfortable, cheap and easily erected homes. The attendees at these regular meetings comprised neighbours and friends, and, if someone could not attend on a particular night, they would ask a neighbour if they wanted to sit in. The host, Mr X., was very particular about the séance protocol; almost regimental. The room in which the séance was held was as dark as possible and it always began with a prayer accompanied by some suitable hymn, or inspirational music. After a very short pause, the next step was always a musical interlude, although not one that you might expect.

Also in the séance room was a radiogram, which played 78 r.p.m. records. Next to it was a piece of furniture with a stack of 78s on it.

The normal procedure was for the sitters to wait until 'spirit' selected a record, which was then – seemingly untouched by human hand – placed on the turntable and the chosen piece of music was heard.

When James Y. attended his first séance there, he was immediately suspicious about the record situation. Yes, he could hear the sound of a record coming out of a sleeve before placement on the turntable, but it all sounded very 'human' to him.

On his next visit he smuggled in a record of his own and surreptitiously placed it in the middle of the stack of records when no one was looking.

The séance began. The normal routine was followed and now it was time for the record. A spirit voice then said, 'Here is one for you James'. Mr Y. then heard the sound of a record being removed from its sleeve and place on the turntable. The music began to play: it was the record that he had brought in with him, "Nymphs and Shepherds" by the Orpheus choir. He was somewhat staggered to say the least. That certainly gave him food for thought.

The meeting continued in the normal manner – spirit voices provided information to the sitters and a materialisation of a figure or figures was sometimes achieved.

As the weeks passed, James became totally convinced about the genuineness of this circle and he continued as a regular sitter. Later, he explained to me that it was, at times, as if the 'space' in the prefab did not exist and that the phenomena did not seem to be contained within the four walls of the room. The sitters would sometimes hear the sound of bagpipes and drums accompanied by the materialisation of a Drum Major in full colourful regalia and staff. He would march up and down the room and throw the staff up in the air to a distance much higher than the height of the ceiling. The staff would fall and he would catch it again throw it up again and so on. Everyone in the room saw the same thing.

I know that it sounds unbelievable but I have no reason to disbelieve this very well educated person, as he had no agenda in giving me this account. Back then I had not written any books and had not thought about doing so.

The next account was given to me by my former colleague Professor Archie Roy. About twenty-five years ago a gentle, older, man from Glasgow came to see Archie and described phenomena that were being achieved in his home circle. Archie had some knowledge of this man and had no reason to disbelieve him. The man and his wife lived in a comfortable red sandstone tenement building consisting of flats, and therefore had neighbours in close proximity.

The man described all sorts of spirit contacts, through a medium and via direct voice. Then, in a matter of fact voice, he said that they were also getting materialisation. Archie was intrigued. The man animatedly explained that, 'A big Spanish wummin' materialised regularly and danced up and down on their dining table, thumping her feet, playing castanets and making a hellova noise'. He said, 'It's great but we need to get rid of her as she is disturbing the neighbours!' The man was most sincere in his giving his account.

I don't know how that all turned out, but I have a lovely mental image of it all; I can almost hear the heel clicks.

Whatever you think of these two accounts, the people providing them had no known mental aberrations and were absolutely sincere in their assertions. Perhaps we may be jealous that we were not there.

And do not let us forget that it was in a private home circle in Glasgow that Arthur Findlay, a prosperous businessman and 'seeker' of religious meaning, became convinced of the reality of an afterlife through the direct voice mediumship of John Sloan. Findlay was from a fairly staunch Christian background but could not quite 'feel' the spirituality in it all. From his conviction, through experiences with Sloan, he became convinced about the continuation of consciousness of those who had passed over. This led him to purchase Stansted Hall in Essex, England as a centre of spiritual education and to author *The Rock of Truth*, *The Edge of the Etheric* and the *Way of Life*, all of which are now classics in the Spiritualist Canon. Arthur was a true gentleman but so convinced was he by the evidence, which he experienced that I believe he became estranged from many members of his family. More correctly, some of his family did not like his new path. But, when you know your truth you can only stick to it; second best is no good if you want to be true to yourself.

I have some home circle photographs from a Springburn group in Glasgow, led by Mr Jim McDonald. A 96 year-old woman who died in 2018 left these to me. As far as I can judge, the photos date from the 1930s and 1940s, maybe earlier. I know no more than that. The lady who passed was nobody's fool and remained as sharp as a tack mentally until she died in 2018. These black and white photos show spirit faces around the medium, and sometimes around the sitters, during the séances. Some images are a bit blurred but others are very clear and I am told that after the photos were developed, the appropriate sitters could recognise the 'extra' people in them perfectly well, whether they were family, friends, neighbours or whoever. I realise that this has no credibility or proof to you as a reader and some of the photos do look so strange that you would have to think that they were fraudulent, but answer me this: these photos have been kept in a drawer for all of these years; no one has tried to bring them forward for fame or fortune during that time; so would it be likely that deliberate fraud would have been perpetrated? To what end? Nobody has made any claims about them. Below are three examples.

As I know the source and credibility of the people involved, I have come to accept them as genuine.

# 11

# Summing Up

What can we make of the accounts in this book? Does it help us to find out who we are, or what talents we may possess? It is life and death, but not as we 'normally' know it.

So there we are. I have provided you with a wide range of phenomena illustrating many bizarre unexplained events that actually happened. Some of these are indicative of survival of our consciousness after shuffling off the mortal coil and others do not necessarily have to invoke a survival hypothesis. But, overall they are very strange and apparently unaccountable happenings. Present day science does not have a model for many of these events but that does not mean that they are not true. We are, indeed, a complex species. I would like to think that these events are natural and do have reason, otherwise it makes no sense as nature doesn't seem to like things that are not useful or make no sense.

I asked the question at the beginning of this book, 'Why do we exist at all?' That I still cannot answer, but let us consider a few things.

The human race's estimate of its own importance in the scheme of things has had to be revised downwards a number of times in recent history. From being a special creation of God in the Universe with the Earth at the centre, it has had to accept that the place it inhabits is one of the smaller planets of a system of bodies orbiting a run-of-the-mill second or third generation star known as the Sun which itself is one of 100,000,000,000 forming a galaxy, that galaxy being only one among at least 10,000,000,000 in the known Universe. For anyone aware of such facts it must have occurred to them that if the human race, and the Earth, and the Solar System *and our entire Galaxy* were annihilated, it would, on a universal scale, be the equivalent of taking out one speck of dust from the 10,000,000,000 floating in the dusty atmosphere within a cathedral.

We also used to think that humans had evolved to a state where we each have the biggest, most powerful and complex brain on the planet. Not so. The brains of whales and dolphins, are as big and, more importantly, as complex as the human brain. Other mammals are undoubtedly intelligent and, if anyone asks where their civilisation is, the answer is that they do not need one as such, as they have adapted to their oceanic environment – unlike we, who have despoiled the Earth with pollution, deep mining, fracking and now, having filled the seas with plastic waste, we are threatening their environment.

It has been argued that what then distinguishes the human race from other inhabitants is its ability to modify the environment, fashion and use tools, and communicate by the use of language. Even there, however, mankind is different only to the extent to which he embraces such activities. Beavers build dams; birds build nests with some species decorating them aesthetically; ants and termites construct nests with some ants even keeping aphids as 'cattle' to 'milk'. Chimpanzees strip the leaves from twigs to winkle ants out from nests, as do some birds. Even language is not the sole distinction that man enjoys. Apart from the natural 'language' of gestures, dances, scents, growls, calls, songs, we now know that apes and chimpanzees can be taught human sign language – even to the extent that some of them will create new "words", including new gestures when angry. And, who knows, as whales and dolphins swim through their oceanic depths, what esoteric realms their minds tune into, or what information or dreams they transmit to each other in their complicated and beautiful songs.

In our defence, we can feel compassion and cry for other human beings whom we do not even know. That empathy must surely mean something.

But human beings have also had to face the additional unwelcome discovery that their brain and personalities might not be in sole control of their thinking processes or body's activities. The researches of Frederick Myers, William James, Sigmund Freud and Carl Gustav Jung, to name a few, showed that a person's conscious personality was not even managing director in the public limited company of his mind but was more aptly described as the public relations officer. The unconscious mind was the portmanteau term coined to embrace all the thought processes, motives, drives and impulses, which the conscious was not aware of. Psychoanalysis, the therapeutic procedure begun and shaped by Freud, Jung, Adler and their followers, had as a goal the bringing into consciousness of unconscious material that was at the back of the patient's illness. To many people, the subconscious was vaguely reminiscent of an attic or cellar in which old junk, no longer wanted, was stored 'out of sight, out of mind', although to some, the unconscious had unpleasant overtones of a nastily clogged drain, capable of causing trouble. The notion that a person possessed a subconscious mind became a 'respectable' idea and part of the accepted world picture of what a human being was. People adjusted to the idea: it then became very acceptable and desirable, and still is, to be 'in therapy', often for years, to clear whatever the subconscious block was that hindered ordinary life.

Is the subconscious his or her servant, normally attending without trouble to the uninteresting but necessary below stairs duties, allowing its owner to get on with all the higher decision-making? The person might not be absolute master or mistress of his or her head but at least it was their own head and no one else's.

But, is that always so?

We have already seen from previous chapters that there are good grounds for believing that the idea of a person being a closed organism with only five senses to the outside world is hopelessly inadequate. Information can become available to a human being, on occasion, that cannot have arrived via these five senses. So must we also consider seriously the proposition that there can be other influences in the mind? Is it possible that under the right circumstances, uninvited entities, benevolent or malevolent, can enter and try, for their own purposes, to influence the person or even dislodge that person and hijack the body? E.g. trance healers; Heydrich; spirit controls. It would seem so.

I believe that the true and bizarre events, which I have told you about, make us entirely different from other species and make us truly unique. With that knowledge should come responsibility for the world, others and, probably more importantly, personal responsibility for our individual thoughts and deeds.

I contend that I have demonstrated to you that we on Earth have an amazing potential to tap into and affect Earthly things, if only we all knew how to maximise it. I have also shown that examples such as Jesse Shepard, EVP and the extraordinary psychic surgeons, show that discarnate conscious beings bring their expertise to the human condition – unless you can provide another explanation, which fits *all* the facts.

This being the case, the evidence for survival of consciousness is strong.

Before you dismiss some of the things that I have told you about, weigh up and study the evidence and know that this book merely touches the edges of many mysteries. My previous books seem somewhat 'normal' compared with this one, as they have included chapters on reasonably well-known and accepted paranormal topics.

You can increase your understanding of any given topic that interests you by further reading. To that end I recommend the use of the bibliography at the end of this book.

Your head may be hurting now, your credulity limit stretched to its limit and some of you will probably be more confused about the paranormal and survival than you were when you started this book. It is not that there is no paranormal activity in the world but probably too much, chiefly because the generalised topic of the 'paranormal' spreads out into so many branches. You must always look at the evidence for the validity of any events, which are claimed within any particular branch that you care to follow. You will have your favourites. There are some people, however, who will not even contemplate examining any paranormal topic because it seems so against anything that they have accepted as reality. They never seem to think that, as described above, the existence of life on Earth is in itself a most peculiar event.

Nobel prize winner Max Plank, generally known as the father of quantum theory, had this to say about life in this material world:

'All matter originates and exists only by virtue of a force'. His conclusion was that, 'We must assume behind this force the existence of a conscious and intelligent mind; this mind is the matrix of all matter'.

You and I may agree or disagree with his conclusion; that is our choice. But one thing that we do know as a certainty is that everything on Earth is made of 'matter'. All matter comprises atoms, which themselves comprise subatomic particles. Bizarrely, and truthfully, it has been shown that each atom comprises mostly empty space and yet everything vibrates and everything vibrates at its own particular frequency.

Quantum Entanglement has been called, 'Spooky action at a distance'. I venture to say that human life could be called, 'Spooky action here and now'.

I have previously written about the quality, intelligence and integrity of brilliant scientists and scholars who have spent an enormous amount of time examining 'paranormal' topics. As already stated, this has been the case since 1882 with the foundation of the Society for Psychical Research in London. These are not topics for cranks, although some of the material that I have shared with you might make you think differently.

Again I stress that you must weigh up the evidential value of the accounts that I have written about and really think about them with a sensible and open mind.

I have been researching these matters for over thirty years, as have hundreds, more probably thousands, of genuine researchers whose only objective is to find out the truth about our human condition.

You only have to look at the bibliography in this book to get the calibre and flavour of a few.

Dr Isaac Funk, D.D., LL.D., co-founder of the publishing company Funk and Wagnall, spent many years investigating aspects of the paranormal and his conclusion was as follows:

'I confess that some of these experiences are so startling that if they had not come within my own vision and hearing, being myself fully acquainted with the details of the test conditions imposed, I should be strongly tempted to doubt them'.

He also wrote: 'No laugh can be loud enough, no sarcasm acidic enough, nor scepticism violent enough, to destroy a fact'.

Professor Henry Sidgwick said:

> The records of experiments must depend ultimately on the probity and intelligence of the persons recording them, and it is impossible for us, as investigators, to demonstrate to persons who do not know us that we are not idiotically careless or consciously mendacious. We can only hope that within the limited circle in which we are known, either alternative will be regarded as highly improbable.

This is where I come in and there IS the nub. I have not spent over thirty years on a whim and wasting my time on nonsense. I look at evidential value.

There is no substitute for experience, or by availing yourself of the best credible literature.

As far as your personal experiences are concerned, the test of any experience is the clarity by which you remember that event. The memory of it should be as clear in every detail ten, twenty, thirty, forty years later, as it was on the day of the event.

Do not let anyone tell you what to think, weigh up the evidence for yourself. I again contend that to anyone with a sensible open mind the evidence shows, 'Beyond any reasonable doubt,' that physical death is not the end of your consciousness, your personality, the real you – whatever you want to call it.

I subscribe to the wisdom of Socrates when he said,

'I cannot teach anybody anything; I can only make them think'.

I have, hopefully, taken you on a journey that makes *you* think, albeit that some of the accounts are, on the face of it, unbelievable and/or bizarre.

I can only inform. Any further inquiry about these matters and other relevant phenomena is up to you, but please also remember that while you are here on Earth this physical life can also be amazing and wondrous.

Enjoy the journey!

# Bibliography

And recommended reading

JSPR/PSPR Journal/Proceedings of the Society for Psychical Research.

JASPR/PASPR Journal/Proceedings of the American Society for Psychical Research.

Alexander, E. 2012 *Proof of Heaven*. Piatkus.

Berger, A.S. 1988. *Evidence for Life After Death: a casebook for the tough minded.*

New York. Charles C Thomas.

Braude, S.E. 2003 *Immortal Remains, The Evidence for Life After Death.* Rowman and Littlefield.

Braude, S.E. *The Gold Leaf Lady,* 2007 University of Chicago Press.

Cardoso, A., The *ITC Journal,* since 2000. Hundreds of articles and editorials.

Cardoso, A., (2010). *Electronic Voices, Contact with Another Dimension*? Ropley, Hants, UK: John Hunt/O-Books.

Cardoso, A., (2012). A Two-Year Investigation of the Allegedly Anomalous Electronic Voices or EVP. *NeuroQuantology* | September 2012 | Volume 10, Issue 3, pp. 492-514.

Cardoso, A., (2017). *Electronic Contact with the Dead, What Do the Voices Tell Us?* Hove, UK: White Crow Books.

Cardoso, A., (2018). *A handbook of EVP,* What you need to know to attempt the electronic contact with the deceased. White Crow Books.

Carr, B.J. 2008 Worlds apart: Can psychical research bridge the gulf between matter and mind? PSPR, 59, 1-96.

Cooper, C., 2012 *Telephone Calls From the Dead.* Tricorn Books.

Cooper, C., 2013 *Conversations With Ghosts,* White Crow Books.

Edwards, H., 1962 *The Mediumship of Jack Webber,* The Healer Publishing Company.

Eisenbud, J., 1968 *The World of Ted Serios,* Pocket Books, New York.

Findlay, Arthur, 1953 *On the Edge of the Etheric, The Rock of Truth, Looking Back, The Way of Life.* WBC Print Ltd.

Fodor, Nandor., 1963 *Between two Worlds,* Parker Publication.

Fontana, D., 1991 A Responsive Poltergeist: a case from South Wales. *JSPR 57,* 385-403.

Fontana, D., 2009 *Life Beyond Death, What Should We Expect?* Watkins Publishing.

Fontana, D., 2006 *Is There an Afterlife,* O Books, Hants.

Fuller, J. G., 1981 *The Airmen Who would not Die,* Corgi, London.

Fuller, J G., 1985 *The Ghost of 29 Megacycles,* Souvenir Press, London.

Fuller, J.G., 1974 *Arigo: Surgeon of the Rusty Knife,* Hart-Davis, MacGibbon.

Gauld, A., 1966-72 A Series of 'Drop-in' Communicators, *PSPR 55, 273-340.*

Gauld, A., 1968 *The Founders of Psychical Research.* London: Routledge and Kegan Paul.

Gauld, A. and Cornell, A.D.1979 *Poltergeists. London and Boston*: Routledge & Kegan Paul.

Gauld, A., 1982. *Mediumship and Survival.* Heinemann, London.

Gurney, E., Myers, F.W.H., and Podmore, F1886. *Phantasms of the Living,* vols. 1 and 2. The Society for Psychical Research and Trubner and Company.

Hamilton, T., 2012 *Tell My Mother I'm not Dead.* Imprint Academic.

Haraldsson, E., 2000 Birthmarks and Claims of Previous-Life Memories. 1. The Case of Purnima Ekanayake. *JSPR, 64.1, 16-25.*

Haraldsson, E., 2013 *The Departed Among The Living.* White Crow Books.

Haraldsson, E. and Stevenson, I. 1975, A Communicator of the 'Drop-in' type in Iceland: The Case of Runolfur Runolfsson. *JASPR 69, 35-59.*

Haraldsson, E. and Stevenson, I. 1975, A Communicator of the 'Drop-in' type in Iceland: The Case of Gudni Magnusson. *JASPR 69, 245-261.*

Hutton J. B., 1978 *Healing Hands.* W.H. Allen.

Hyslop, J.H., 1909. A Case of Veridical Hallucinations, *PASPR 3, 1-469.*

Inglis, Brian, 1977 *Natural and Supernatural,* Hodder and Stoughton.

Inglis, Brian, 1984 *Science and Parascience,* Hodder and Stoughton.

Inglis, Brian, 1985 *The Paranormal,* Granada, London.

Ireland, M., 2010 *Soul Shift.* Frog Books.

Ireland, M., 2013 *Messages From The Afterlife,* North Atlantic Books, California.

Lodge, O., 1909 *Survival of Man,* Methuen, London.

Lodge, O., Evidence of Classical Scholarship and of Cross-Correspondence in some New Automatic Writing. *PSPR 25,129-142.*

Mackenzie, A., 1971 *Apparitions and Ghosts.* Arthur Barker, London.

Margolis, J., 1998 *Uri Geller, Magician or Mystic?* Orion Books Ltd, London.

Oaten, E. W., 1928 *The Chaffin Will Case.* Manchester. The Two Worlds Publishing Company.

Peake, A., 2010, *Is There Life after Death?,* Arcturus Publishing Ltd.

Piper, A. L., 1929 *The Life and Work of Mrs. Piper.* London: Kegan Paul.

Playfair, G. L., 1975 *The Flying Cow,* Souvenir Press, also known as the following:

Playfair, G.L. 1977 *The Unknown Power,* Panther Books Ltd.

Playfair, G. L., 2011 *This House is Haunted,* White Crow Books, Guildford.

Playfair, G. L., and Grosse, M. 1988 Enfield Revisited, *JSPR 55, 50-78.*

Playfair, G. L., 2012 *Twin Telepathy.* White Crow Books, Guildford.

Playfair, G. L., 2011 *Chico Xavier, Medium of the Century.* Roundtable publishing.

Pollack, Jackson H., 1966 *Croiset the Clairvoyant,* A Mayflower-Dell. Psychic Press. 1979 *The Teachings of Silver Birch.*

Raudive, K., 1971 *Breakthrough,* Gerrards Cross: Colin Smythe.

Richet, C., 1923. Thirty Years of Psychical Research: Being a Treatise on *Metapsychics* (S. de Brath, Trans.) New York: MacMillan.

Robertson, T. J., 2013, *Things You Can Do When You're Dead,* White Crow Books.

Robertson, T. J., 2015 *More Things You Can do when You're Dead,* White Crow Books.

Robertson, T. J. and Roy, *A.E.*2001, A preliminary Study of the Acceptance by Non-Recipients of Mediums' Statements to Recipients. *JSPR 65.2 91-106.*

Roy A. E. and T. J. Robertson 2001, A Double Blind Procedure for assessing The Relevance of a Medium's Statements to a Recipient .*JSPR 65.3 161-74.*

Robertson T. J. and Roy A.E. 2004, Results of the Application of the Robertson-Roy. Protocol to a series of Experiments with Mediums and Participants. *JSPR 68.1 18-34.*

Rogo, D. Scott, 1979 *The Poltergeist Experience.* Penguin books, Baltimore (USA).

Rogo, D. Scott, 1988 *The Infinite Boundary.* The Aquarian Press: Wellingborough.

Roy, A. E., 1996 *The Archives of the Mind.* Psychic Press, Stansted.

Roy, A.E., 2008. *The Eager Dead,* Book Guild.

Sartori, P., 2014 *The Wisdom of Near Death Experiences,* Watkins.

Stemman, R., 1971 *Medium Rare, biography of Ena Twigg,* S.A.G.B.

Stemman, R., 1998, *Reincarnation: true stories of Past Lives.* Piatkus.

Stemman, R., 2012 *The Big Book Of Reincarnation,* Hierophant Publishing.

Stemman, R., 2017 Updated version, *Surgeon From Another World.* White Crow Books.

Stevenson, I., 1972 Are Poltergeists Living or are They Dead? *JASPR66, 233 - 252.*

Stevenson, I., 1974 *Twenty Cases Suggestive of Reincarna*tion, University of Virginia Press, Charlottesville.

Stevenson, I., 1975 Cases of the Reincarnation Type. Vol. 1. Ten Cases in India. Charlottesville: University Press of Virginia.

Stevenson, I., 1977 Cases of the Reincarnation Type. Vol. 2. Ten Cases in Sri Lanka. Charlottesville: University Press of Virginia.

Stevenson, I., 1980 *Cases of the Reincarnation Type. Vol. 3. Twelve Cases in Lebanon and Turkey.* Charlottesville: University Press of Virginia.

Stevenson, I., 1987 *Children Who Remember Previous Lives.* Charlottesville: University Press of Virginia.

Swain, J. 1983 *On the Death of My Son.* Turnstone Press Ltd.

Tucker, J., 2014 *Return to Life.* St Martin's Press, New York.

Twigg E., 1973 *The Woman Who Stunned The World,* Manor Books Inc.

Wickland C., *Thirty Years Among the Dead.* White Crow Books.

Wilson, C., 1982 *Poltergeist,* New English Library, London.

Zammit, V. and W., 2013 *A Lawyer Presents the Evidence for the Afterlife.* White Crow Books.

## About The Author

A former teacher of mathematics and physics, Tricia was a long-term council member of the Scottish Society for Psychical Research. Having been a member of the original council, she held consecutively the positions of Treasurer, Secretary, Vice President and President of this Society.

She was also a tutor for the Department of Adult and Continuing Education (DACE) at the University of Glasgow. In conjunction with Professor Archie Roy she provided latterly a session programme of twenty, two hour, lectures per session in a series entitled "An In-Depth Study of Psychical Research". An earlier course was entitled "An Introduction to Psychical Research". These courses covered many topics and ran for six years examining, in essence, 'The paranormal-what is the evidence?'

In addition to over 30 years of experience in investigating spontaneous cases, Tricia has appeared on various TV programmes, usually documentaries, and on radio programmes including America's *Coast to Coast*, twice, UK's Radio City, USA Darkness Radio, Celtic Radio, Beyond 3D, Hayhouse Radio, Past Lives Podcast, Talk Radio and The unexplainedtv.com, many times. Nowadays she is also invited to speak in various Zoom meetings and blogs throughout the U.K., U.S.A., Australia and Holland. These invitations continue.

She wrote the foreword to Mark Ireland's highly successful book *Soul Shift* and has text included in his second book *Messages from the Afterlife*. Along with this she has written an endorsement for The Galilean Pendulum and some of her comments are on the back cover of Trevor Hamilton's book *Tell my Mother I am not Dead*.

Tricia is known as an interesting and exciting speaker on many topics concerning psychical research, which is reflected by the invitations that she receives from varied organisations, including various Psychical Research Societies in the UK and abroad, Associations for Spiritual Knowledge, Mensa at Malvern, Alternative Perspectives, The Glastonbury Symposium, Glasgow University Clubs, The Churches Fellowship for Spiritual and Psychic Studies, The Quakers, The Unitarian Church and the Open University.

## *Research*

Along with the many television and radio appearances plus hands on research she has also prepared and presented many papers to the SPR and other International Conferences.

She and Professor Archie Roy are co-authors of three peer reviewed published papers on the study of the accuracy of information provided by mediums. These papers follow the progress of a five-year study of controlled experiments, which were conducted in conditions up to triple blinding. The results of these studies are published in the Journal of the Society for Psychical Research (JSPR) April 2001, January 2004 and July 2004.

Tricia was also a founding member and Hon Sec of PRISM, Psychical Research Involving Selected Mediums, 1994-2008. Other members of PRISM included Professor Arthur Ellison, Professor David Fontana, Professor Archie Roy, Philip Holborn, Maurice Grosse and, latterly, Guy Lyon Playfair.

She has also completed a four/five year in-depth study of exceptional ostensible paranormal healing, which began in 2006 and produced some very interesting results. Some of these results would appear to indicate a form of psychic surgery.

The final report concerning this work, entitled *Ostensible Paranormal Healing,* may be downloaded from her website. www.tricarobertson.weebly.com

Along with this work she has also completed and presented a report on a six-year old boy in Scotland who, from when he could speak, remembered details of a previous life. In fact he was extremely vocal about it.

Apart from the three published peer reviewed papers in the JSPR, she has articles published in many journals including the journals of the Swedish and Norwegian Societies for Psychical Research.

Tricia is passionate about the best evidence gathered from various aspects of Psychical Research and does not suffer fools gladly who will not address specific points of evidence in any particular avenue. Her attitude is 'By all means have an opinion, but make it an informed one'.

She states that, 'While accepting that some people may be deluded in their interpretation of some aspects of experience, it is absolutely certain that there are genuine cases within nearly every aspect of paranormal claims, whether they illustrate survival or not'.

Tricia assures us that there is a wealth of evidence out there, which leads her to the conclusion that survival of consciousness would undeniably be the most parsimonious and best explanation for much of the phenomena. The evidence is there for those who really want to read about it and process it with an open mind. This may, hopefully, lead her readers to alter their perception of what may be possible in this world – and perhaps the next.

www.ingramcontent.com/pod-product-compliance
Lightning Source LLC
LaVergne TN
LVHW051001080826
845145LV00009B/2400

* 9 7 8 1 7 8 6 7 7 1 4 3 8 *